To Christopher
Be great!
Larry

CLOSE THE DEAL
By Larry Brooks

A catalogue record for this book is available from the British Library

First Edition published Sept 2010 by KCJ Publishing, Slough. UK.
Email enquiries: kcjpublishing@gmail.com

Cover: www.studio–baker.co.uk

ISBN No: 978-0-9566843-0-1

Printed in England by Think Ink
11-13 Philip Road, Ipswich, Suffolk, IP2 8BH.

To order books go to www.larrybrooks.co.uk

Foreword

I call this my '40 – 40 – 40' book. It took 40 days to write, 40 hours to polish (edit, proof and design) but 40 years hard work and experience to learn exactly what to write!!

I decided to write the book for three main reasons:

Firstly, not only do I have 40 years of work experience and success behind me, but I have seen many of the greatest sales people and trainers in action at live seminars. I have watched all the top DVDs, listened to the best CDs and read the important books. **Success needs to be passed on.**

Secondly, although I have seen some that had a natural flair for selling many just didn't. And it is so frustrating watching so many people make the same mistakes again and again when most of the time they just didn't understand the philosophies and skills involved; more importantly they did not realise that **these skills can be learned.**

Thirdly, I have trained people myself. Every time I saw someone great speaking or training I learned something. I try to help others learn things too; I have taught and coached thousands of people face to face.
Now it was time for a new medium.

So that led me to write this book - a simple and easy-to-understand guide on 'pitching and closing' the deal. The book that would let the everyday person with no real sales skills become a true professional if they followed the contents and learned how to use the information it contained.

I recommend you read it and then work with a 'practice buddy' until you are confident you are 'pitching and closing' correctly in any situation. The confidence you will gain will astound you. You will have learned to 'Close the Deal', whatever the situation.

The Sales Profession is a great club, you should be proud to be a member. I know I am.

Larry

ACKNOWLEDGEMENTS

There are so many people who are and have been an integral part of my life and therefore contributed to this book.

My wife Jose, who is with me all the way, supports me but is never afraid to tell me when I get it wrong. Jose is my Team, the person who makes sure everything around me works OK.

Kaitlyn, my beautiful granddaughter, who only has to smile to light up my day. She has shown me what true caring is, and how real thoughtfulness makes so much difference.

My grandson Connor, a great boy who has boundless energy and a desire to learn and achieve. He makes me see the world though young eyes and learn all over again. He is fun.

Chris Woollams for his friendship and candour. I can always rely on Chris. He corrected and advised on this book. Chris is the closest thing I have to a brother.

Caroline Cary who helped bring out the softer side in me, and the way I work with people. My sister.

Sue and Nigel Booth great friends who patiently read, re–read and corrected every page of this book.

Clive Aroskin. In our twenty year friendship I have watched him continually learn and grow. Clive is my adopted son and his is the final proof you are about to read.

Mike Finding who is responsible for all the web technology. Mike is an important part of Team Larry.

CLOSE THE DEAL

That's what it all comes down to in the end, bringing the conversation to a close with the outcome you wanted.

Closing the Deal does not mean becoming a 'hard nosed salesperson' in fact it is quite the opposite. Calm, quiet confidence because you know what you are doing, rubs off on your customer or any other person you want to close.

Don't however expect everything to go your way. The other person may have objections to your wishes or have their own wish list that conflicts in some way. That's when you 'really earn the money', the time when you have to have strategies ready to make sure the result ends up being satisfactory.

Planning ahead makes all the difference and becoming more knowledgeable and skilled can make that 'razor's edge' difference and mean greater successes.

Closing is not about winning. If there is a winner there must be a loser and that cannot be a healthy situation. It would most certainly mean that your 'opponent', (if you make it about winning and losing then their must be an opponent) will look to redress the balance as quickly as they can and your agreement will soon become worthless.

The ancient Chinese had a great philosophy.

When two people sit down to agree a deal then the deal must end up being good for both of them. That way the two parties can form a long term relationship and a basis for future dealings.

Look at closing as a natural conclusion to any conversation aimed at reaching an agreement or at worse drawing a line.

PART ONE

BECOME A DISCIPLINED PROFESSIONAL

WHY THE PROFESSIONAL GETS PAID AND THE AMATEUR DOES IT FOR NOTHING

IN ANY PROFESSION, YOU WOULD EXPECT TO LEARN THE BASIC FUNDAMENTALS AND UNDERSTAND THE RULES OF ENGAGEMENT. SELLING AND CLOSING ARE NO DIFFERENT; EACH HAS ITS OWN SKILLS AND PHILOSOPHIES, WHICH NEED TO BE ACQUIRED AND LEARNED.

CHAPTER ONE

THE THREE BASIC RULES FOR SUCCESS.

1 BE AN ACTIVE LISTENER.

You cannot argue with nature. We were born with two ears and one mouth and they really should be used in that proportion.

Whenever two or more people talk, new ideas will eventually cross the ether. If you are doing all the talking, how can you ever learn anything from this conversation?

Imagine being a fly on the wall when you have left the situation and you can listen to the way people refer to you. If you have dominated the conversation, more often than not their feelings are that they were overpowered, no one listened to them and they feel unsatisfied.

Now try a conversation that begins with you asking them about them. They will open up to you and talk and talk. The person sitting opposite you is the world's leading expert on their specialist subject – themselves! So sit back and listen.

When they are ready to listen and discuss the reason you are with them, they will be relaxed and happy to talk openly and truthfully. It's amazing the information they will share.

Ask questions then listen to the answers – you will learn an abundance of new ideas.

Simple equation

If the two of us sat down with a good idea in mind, and we shared those ideas, each would walk away with two ideas and be richer for the experience. If it is only me who talks, then I cannot possibly hear your idea and I will not have gained anything. Just imagine, every conversation is building your memory bank and you have a fantastic computer in your head – never miss an opportunity.

You will need to learn how to use all three of the ways we receive information. Auditory, Visual and Kinesthetic.

Some people will take in information more effectively when you talk and they listen. They need to hear it: **Auditory.**

Others will be more receptive if you show them with illustrations or you write out the information and show it to them. They need to see it: **Visual.** Use phrases such as "Can you see what I mean?"

Very often if someone is visual, talking simply won't get the job done, you need to use visual aids too.

Others need to feel it. What is important to them is how they feel about the information you are sharing with them and equally important is how they perceive the way you feel about what you are saying or sharing: **Kinesthetic.** Ask them, "How do you feel about that?" Involve them.

Now is a good time to establish their strongest link. Be aware of their reactions when you speak, take notes or show them a picture and see which is the most effective.

2 Selling isn't Telling, it's Asking

The thinking behind this statement is simple. If you want to sell successfully and consistently, then keep asking questions and listening to the answers. Make sure you remember those answers, they are important. It is always a good idea to keep a pad and pen handy – jot down the major points, it shows you are interested in them and keeps a record for you to use as a checklist when you are closing the deal.

There is a great phrase, *"people don't care what you know, they want to know that you care!"* Show you care about them by asking questions, and mean it. People buy benefits and not features. They don't want to know how their TV works, they want to see that it delivers a great picture quality. They want to know what benefits the major features deliver.

You need to discover what benefits are important to them to ensure you major on those that interest them and why they will gain by owning this product. Note I said owning not buying. No one really wants to be sold anything, nor do they necessarily want to buy, but they are interested in *owning*.

By taking notes, it demonstrates that what they have to say is important to you. Reinforce that by nodding as you write. Ask questions to let them reiterate their major points and you will be amazed at how warm they become.

This is not a 'trick'. Remember when you strike any deal it has to be good for both sides, so be aware of their 'wants.'

3 TELL THE TRUTH

Know your products or service and the benefits they provide. Know how and why they deliver those benefits.

Then make sure you answer any question confidently and truthfully . If you are not sure – *tell the truth* – and say so. Your prospect will always have more respect for you if you demonstrate that you are not simply a know it all and perhaps spreading that brown stuff that comes out of bulls.

Great selling is a craft like any other. When people say they don't like sales people they normally mean the poor ones. The pushy ones who will not listen and just keep pushing for the deal *they* want and not one their customer needs or wants.

They simply don't listen. They dive into a presentation without asking any questions and that becomes a 'hard sell'.

Their customers don't buy. They don't sell. Their customer doesn't like sales people and they don't like '*Not selling*'

How many times have you heard someone say "But I don't like selling." That is not what they really mean.

Actually what they don't like is NOT SELLING. Who does? What they dislike and cannot handle is rejection. The fact that someone says "No" to them. When they get a 'No' they try to get someone to change their mind and they see that as the 'hard sell'

They don't like 'the hard sell' but are OK with the 'soft sell.'

CHAPTER TWO

WHAT IS HARD SELL OR SOFT SELL?

I find this interesting. Ask yourself the question "what is the difference between hard sell and soft sell?"

Most people have an opinion but aren't really sure, and yet the answer is really very simple .If you think that hard sell is applying pressure in order to sell then soft sell must be not applying any pressure.

Selling is the art of professional persuasion.

The people that sold Margaret Thatcher to the majority of voters were sales people.

When Margaret Thatcher got everyone behind the Falklands War that was selling. Most didn't even know where the Falkland Islands were but she invoked a passion in us.

When the Army runs a recruitment campaign and a young person walks into a recruitment office, that's selling.

Without some pressure, people will revert to type – and everyone finds it easier to do nothing than make the effort to invoke a change. Nothing will happen, so what was the point? People find it just as hard to say "No" as they do to say "Yes." It is making a decision they have trouble with.

There is one way where you don't seem to apply any pressure. In a perfect world you have a pre–planned energised, mini–presentation to deliver information about an Opportunity, Product, Service, Idea etc. that the person would then be interested in because it will deliver a benefit that would suit them. They want to do the deal. That is selling!

The girl on the checkout at the supermarket wouldn't call herself a salesperson and neither would most people describe her as one. Yet here is the reality.

The supermarket sets out their store. More people drive by than come in (Rejection)
You enter the store. You walk past more products than you select (Rejection) you can even put some back if you like (Rejection) but then you come to the checkout.

The girl turns into a 'closer'. Do you have a loyalty card? (Close) You say "Yes" then you are buying. She swipes the goods and then says £76.41 (Close). You place your card in the reader and enter your pin. Her 'selling you' the price was a 'close', but because you wanted what you have in your trolley there doesn't appear to be any pressure.

You see, if you can supply what your prospect wants at a price they can afford and they believe is value for money, a sale will take place. Your description and help in their deciding to buy is 'professional persuasion' not pressure. Be honest and warm and people will hear what you say and want what you have to offer. That is selling.

Even if you want to sell online without any live conversation, you need to carefully plan the headlines and contents of each page otherwise your site will not produce sales. Then you would put in 'click throughs' and 'next buttons' which will lead the person to the checkout and payment (Close).

Try to talk, without planning what you are going to say, about an idea that you have no idea whether it will suit the person you are talking to. You are haphazard, lethargic. When they say "I am not interested," then when pressed by you, give an excuse, you try to deal with that excuse (which you have wrongly labelled as an objection). Then the more you try, the more pointless it becomes and the person feels under pressure to stop the conversation – so they do.
That leaves you with a feeling of rejection or frustration and that isn't pleasant. I wouldn't want that feeling and that is

the emotion that so many people who are lacking understanding and knowledge of this communication skill, experience. It's no wonder they don't like selling.

So why not change the outcome by training, as any craftsman or sportsman would do? Train to become fit and rehearsed until the action becomes 'natural' and everything keeps happening the way it was planned and results become more positive, more often.

You will then have those quick answers to hand and stop that frustration of 'if only.'

Find a role model, someone you respect and has great results; a person that you want to emulate. When I was a child, I had sportsmen who played the games I loved and they were my heroes. Role models and that helped me improve my game by watching them and trying to follow their lead.

Do the same and use the ideas and habits that they display to develop your 'game.' Then you will find yourself evolving with your own style and standards of expertise. Everything in this book can become a learned skill. The only differences between the very best and the raw beginner are the desire to become number one and practice.

Practice, practice, practice is the mantra. Make sure that the closes become second nature to you. On the back of well delivered presentations they are dynamite and provided you stick to the truth and don't make wild promises, can earn you a fortune.

Of course the best close of all is a well delivered presentation to a qualified prospect who, at the end – asks you if they can have the proposition and the deal closes itself.

You can experience that too if you really want.

CHAPTER THREE

USE OPEN QUESTIONS

WHO – HOW – WHAT – WHERE – WHEN?

Start by making this a sales conversation. Ask questions that prompt more than a one word answer. I mean don't ask "How long have you lived here?" which prompts a short sharp answer of perhaps "Five years," ask "Who saw the house first?" "How did you find this great house?" Be ready to follow up with "Where did you move from?" Get them used to talking. Let them gain their confidence while you show genuine interest. After all you want to know what they think and how they feel.

It is amazing how right we are when, we, the customer, speak. Your customers are the worlds leading experts on themselves. They know their subject inside out. Give your customers the chance and they will tell you exactly what you need to do to close the deal with them.

Your children are no different. The times I hear parents saying "My child won't listen to me" yet they don't take the time to listen to their child. Wives will say the same of their husbands and employees of their bosses. Listen and learn!

Start to observe other people when they meet in a social environment. It is amazing how many just want to talk about themselves. They never take the time to listen to the other person and yet that is so rewarding in more ways than one. If you will sit back and listen to them they will like you. They want to be heard. Show interest and gain friends. People buy from people they like and have an empathy with.

These five words can stimulate every conversation you will ever need, make them your friends and use them

Plan your Presentation – A Story

Jack, a Life Insurance Salesman has managed to get an appointment with a Sales Manager of a company and calls to see him in his office with a view to selling him a policy.

His opening line is, "I don't suppose you really want any life insurance do you?" to which the Sales Manger becomes wide eyed and incredulous.

"You cannot possibly begin a presentation like that," he says. "Look, let me show you" and taking the Jack's presenter, proceeds to teach him what a structured, prepared sales presentation looks like.

The Sales Manager is a 'natural teacher' and cannot resist helping someone who doesn't appear to have any idea of how to deliver an effective presentation.

At the end, the Jack asks if he would have bought following a presentation of that nature and the Sales Manager says "Yes of course." The sale is then closed and as Jack packs his case and starts to leave, the Sales Manger says "Now that is what you call a planned, effective sales presentation."

Jack replies "And you have just seen my planned, prepared, sales presentation for Sales Managers."

PLAN YOUR PRESENTATION.

The best and most effective presentation is one that closes itself; in other words your prospect says, "I want that now" and everything is so easy. When that fails to happen, it will normally raise objections – their reasons not to say yes – and they will fall into three categories:

1. The items important to them which you have failed to satisfy them on during the presentation.
2. The items you haven't covered at all and,
3. The insincere objections they will raise simply because they think they should say something or they want to delay making a decision. Planning your presentation will define which category their objection falls into.

Your presentation should follow a pattern.
Step One: People buy people first, so make sure you give them good reason to warm to you and trust you immediately.

Step two: build the same trust in your company and its' integrity and values.

Step three: make sure you demonstrate the advantages and benefits that they would enjoy by owning your product or using your service.

Step four: qualify your prospect. Is this the product they want and if the price is OK would they buy it now?

They will either say "Yes" or give you an objection, and this is great, you can now qualify precisely by asking "Is that the only reason?" Ignore it, then carry on with pricing.
You are now in a position to close effectively. If you fail to do this then anything can happen because you left the door wide open. Make sure what you need to do is always clear to you.

Think of making a sale as walking down a corridor in a hotel. There are rooms every few feet and each room contains a feature and benefit that you need to deliver to your prospect. You are going to gently lead them down the hall and open each door, show them what's inside and then when they are satisfied, CLOSE EACH DOOR.

Along the corridor there are fire doors which need to be CLOSED for your safety. There is one at the end of each section of your presentation but the door will not close until you have checked and CLOSED every room door. Every time you CLOSE a fire door you have sealed the rear exit and there is only one way out and that is moving forward.

Finally, there is a stretch of corridor beyond the last fire door with no other rooms off to the side, simply two final doors facing you at the end of the hall.

One is marked "Yes" the other is marked "No".

Your goal is to get your prospect through one of the doors. You influence their choice by highlighting what is behind each door. If they choose the Yes door they gain all the advantages and benefits they wanted you to provide. If they choose the No door they walk away with nothing.

Imagine you have been gently but firmly, leading them all the way until you pass the final 'fire door' when you step to one side and their momentum carries them past you. Now you block the way back, effectively 'closing' the escape route. The only way out is through either the Yes or No door and that is your goal. You want a clear decision so that you can move on. I know you would rather have the Yes, but No will be OK, it just cannot be left undecided or you cannot be fully focussed on your next sale. You will be distracted and that spells disaster.

Remember - all distractions are equal. Stay focussed.

CHAPTER FOUR

WHAT IS CLOSING?

Well, it is exactly what it sounds. Towards the end of this pre–planned presentation there needs to be a point where the conversation is brought to a close. Simple!

Where does the phrase come from? In the early days of modern direct selling, canvassers or Openers worked door to door to generate enquiries. The Closer would sit in his car at the end of the road whilst his team of two canvassers or Openers would cold call and then start the presentation to establish interest. When the prospect qualified, they would call in the Closer to wrap up, or close the deal.
Hence the name, Closer.

The Opener had a very precisely rehearsed presentation so that the Closer could continue knowing exactly what had been covered during the Opener's presentation or pitch.

The Opener would qualify the prospect by introducing them to the Closer in a specific way. For example: " Mr and Mrs Jackson, this is Mr Arnold Brown who is the Area Manager for Countywide Kitchens who will be able to help you out."

"Mr Brown, Mr and Mrs Jackson are interested in a new kitchen for their home but are concerned as to the price. Is that right Mr Jackson?" When Mr Jackson agreed (and why not) he was perfectly set up for qualification and close.
The Closer would continue the pitch; demonstrate the product and show samples. Qualify it was what they wanted, then deliver the price and close the deal.

Parents do the same. The child wants to do something that Mum or Dad disagrees with. They would both say "No" and Mum knows that.

Mum explains to her child why he or she cannot do this and the answer is "No." The child will argue again so the Mum calls in Dad. Dad now becomes the Closer. He wraps up the conversation by reiterating everything Mum has said. Easy!

OK that's closing in a sales environment but we are all selling all the time. You got your present job by selling yourself at the interview. You got the interview helped by selling yourself on the CV you produced. That CV was a planned presentation.

It is the same when you first asked your girlfriend or boyfriend out. You picked your time, mentally rehearsed what you were going to say then risked rejection You delivered your mini–presentation, asked the closing question and off you went!

Even earlier than that, as a young child you learned to ask things of your parents in a certain way that improved your chances of success.

Every parent knows that when their youngster begins a question with a smile and "Mummy………" or "Daddy …………." in a tone of voice guaranteed to make you go soft inside, that you are going to be asked for something. And doesn't it feel great?

In fact it goes further. Tommy is five. He wants an ice cream. If the answer is "No," he will ask sweetly for the ice cream. He will ask again and again hoping you will give in. If that fails he will promise you the earth if he can have an ice cream. If that fails he will cry and try to make you feel awful for saying no. If that fails he will be naughty in the hope that you will bribe him back into good behaviour by giving him an ice cream. That's selling!

Then the moment he gets the ice cream, he wants a toy.

You see it wasn't the ice cream that was important, Tommy just wanted to see if it worked and then he wanted to try again. He is developing.

Then something awful happens. His parents start telling him all the wrong things.

Shut Up. Speak when you are spoken to. Be quiet when I am speaking. Don't interrupt that's rude and so on. Then when the parents are watching TV and Tommy talks he is told to keep quiet, they are watching this programme. Then, the tables are reversed. Tommy is watching his programme and the adults all talk. They may even tell him to turn the sound down. Is it any wonder that Tommy is confused?

It gets worse. We have the British mentality. Don't cause a fuss, don't send anything back in a restaurant, never query the price, never ask for a discount (only snobs buy retail by the way) and wait your turn in a queue. Is it any wonder we don't have that 'get ahead attitude' that other cultures have. Let's change that right now. Let's be politely more assertive.

Start getting the results you want without walking all over people, in fact they will respect you for your clarity and genuine desire to achieve.

If you read this book, practice the contents and use what you have learned, you will see your results can go through the roof. If you have a team of people you work with then get them to read it too and you will collectively grow and grow with results to match. More importantly you will start to enjoy the experiences and look forward to the next challenge.

Let's first talk about the skills you need in a sales scenario, then we can adapt them for social purposes and occasions.

MINI – PRESENTATIONS

So many people say they can't sell. It simply is not true. Anyone can! All you need is practice which leads to confidence and then you will start to smile and enjoy yourself and that provides the platform for the enthusiasm that will get you the result you are looking to achieve.

These are mini–presentations but they need to take the form of conversations, not monologues. That's why no one can write an effective 'sales script' because your prospect will not have a copy and cannot follow the lines. By using a planned structured conversation you can keep everything moving towards the end result you want to achieve.

There are simple tasks you need to undertake. Don't move on to the next section without completing the task – and no cheating!

Now here is a question for you:

CAN YOU SELL?

Complete the task on the next stage before you go on any further and then you will know whether you can sell or not.

TASK

Prove that you are capable of delivering a presentation aloud. Stand in front of a mirror and say aloud, your full name address, post code and telephone number.

Now think back to when you first moved to this home. You didn't know it. You had to write your post code down and refer to it when asked, just in the same way as your telephone number didn't roll off your tongue in the early days.

Continuous repetition and use means that now, you know it off by heart. Practice and use made it readily available.

Now, I want you to deliver the directions to your home from the nearest roundabout.

That means you need to visualise the roundabout, then drive the route in your mind and, as you do, write it down so that you can read it out loud to the mirror. Read it again and again until you know it without looking at the 'script.'

Well done – you CAN deliver an effective presentation.

That means --------You can sell.

Now you need to learn mini – presentations and become comfortable using them in order to close the deals.

Here is a thought. How would you like to never have someone say No to you again, in a way that causes you to feel rejected and unloved?

Ok, that's a great goal to strive for and when you master the mini–presentations and develop a feeling for the sales process You will never take rejection personally again.

That is my promise to you.

You must have experienced that wonderful feeling of satisfaction when you have completed a job that you are really proud of. It was as simple as cutting the lawn with a great stripe effect and then finishing it off by trimming the edges and getting rid of all the cuttings. It looked great.

I have news for you. It will grow again. It will change, but the way you felt right then was worth all the effort.

Perhaps you took the time to take your child to the adventure playground he loves to play in. You saw the joy in his face.

You went fishing together and watched them learn a new skill and the joy of joys they got a bite and landed a fish. They want to do it again and again – why? Because it felt great.

On another occasion, there might not have been the bites but that was OK because you had a great time and had the chance to share the experience. You see, it is not always just winning that matters.

When you can walk away from a prospect without a deal, but you know you have done everything you could to the very best of your ability, then you wont get that same feeling of rejection and you realise it is not personal – they just didn't buy what you had to sell. Next!

PART TWO

UNDERSTANDING CLOSING

CLOSING IS AN ART,
PHRASES DELIVERED WITH
FINESSE AND TIMING

There is a simple rule when closing.

When you ask a closing question
SHUT UP
and listen to the answer

CHAPTER FIVE

WHAT IS A CLOSING QUESTION, A CLOSE?

Any question to which a definite answer is requested, will denote the state of the deal at that time.

They are deliberately phrased questions, which fall into three categories depending on how and why they are used. It can be the same question to test the water, set up a final close or precede a final closing question.

1. THE TRIAL CLOSE?

A question delivered during the pitch just to test that you are on the right track. If you have divided your presentation into parts, for example Company, Product, and Price, then at the end of each section you could ask a closing question to test and ensure whether that particular part has been covered to your prospect's satisfaction. These Trial Closes also therefore act as Qualifying Questions and allow you to move forward knowing you have effectively 'closed the door' on everything so far.

Examples. " So are you confident that Cuisine Kitchens are the right people to build and install your new kitchen?"

"Are you totally happy with that style and finish for your kitchen and the appliances tick all your boxes?"

Now you can move on and price with confidence.

2. An Intermediate Close?

A question delivered to see how close to a deal you have become. The great thing about using these, often linked closes is that you never again need ask the final closing question without first knowing that the answer will be the one you want to hear. Imagine – no more rejection.

3. A Final Close

This is exactly what it says. When you ask this question you are expecting to close the deal. If the answer is affirmative then the deal is done. If the answer is "No," it will become an objection and you will read later in this book exactly how to turn an objection into an opportunity to close again and that means repeating the final closing question or using a different one.

Notice that Closes are all questions not statements.

For a close to be effective, it must end with a closing question. Why? For the very simple reason that a close leads to a response, a statement leads to silence. You need an answer, therefore you need to ask the question then listen.

You will solicit a positive answer or a reason why your prospect is not inclined to proceed. It is termed an objection which can then be used to move forward.

When should you start Closing?

The golden rule is start closing sooner rather than later. Use Trial Closes as early on in the pitch as you can, then keep testing the temperature of the water. Getting a yes will give you encouragement and a no will let you cover the point or leave it as an objection until later. You cannot lose by closing.

What is an Objection?

Most people consider objections as stumbling blocks between you and the deal. That is one way of viewing them, but it is a view that will not bring success. When the objection is genuine, then it indicates the challenge or challenges between you and the deal you want to close.

To the professional, an objection is any question or statement that when correctly handled gives you the opportunity to ask a closing question. Objections will indicate your level of progress and you need that so that you know exactly what's left to achieve. So objections are friends not foe. Most people treat objections as the enemy but you will see later on, that they are one of your greatest assets.

What is a Condition?

This is a state where your prospect has for example, no means to pay and you can't provide one. They cannot use your product (you are selling meat and they are vegetarian.) In other words, you are totally incompatible and there is absolutely no point in delivering a presentation to them. If you are sure a genuine condition exists then get out of there; you simply don't have a viable prospect and there is absolutely no point in continuing with the presentation.

If it ever happens, make sure you question them, "Why are we discussing this when it doesn't fit your criteria?" Find out and you may see it disappear. Always check it out.

Task

Write a list of conditions under which the best sales person in the world could not sell. This is harder than you think!

I will start you off – Your prospect is dead!

CHAPTER SIX

PREPARE YOURSELF

Make sure before you enter into any negotiation or sales arena that you are fully prepared for almost all eventualities.

When I was 'on the road' as a direct salesman, I used to carry a spare shirt and tie just in case I spilt coffee when I was with a client and then had to go on to the next appointment.

Do you need support documentation (there is a great saying that 'Documentation beats Conversation') and would illustrations or pictures help?
Remember a picture is worth a thousand words.

Have you prepared your presentation and rehearsed it? Practice with a friend or practice buddy; don't practice on your live prospect – they are too valuable. No actor or performer would dream of attempting to deliver a show without adequate rehearsal.
Warm up on the way there. Sing in the car. Go through your opening presentation.

All these things switch your mind on and you are ready to hit the ground running as your presentation begins.

You only get one chance to make a first impression.

QUALIFY YOUR PROSPECT

By this I mean, can you close a deal with this person here and now? I don't mean you will, only that you could.

For example; "Tom, you and Mary are looking for a new sofa. Is there an event coming up that you wanted the sofa for?" Tom says "No, but we are redecorating and re–carpeting in six to eight weeks time, and want the sofa to finish everything off." Now you have a qualifying factor.

"In that case Tom, as delivery is normally eight weeks and some are longer, can I suggest I point out those that would fit that delivery time?" Tom says "Great."

"Can I ask then Tom if we can find a sofa you like, at a price that fits your budget, can we process everything today to achieve that delivery time. Is that OK with you?" Tom agrees. He is a qualified prospect. If he says "no", then just move on; ignore it and you can try again later, but know that you cannot try to close this deal until he becomes qualified. Let's use Tom and Mary as our example – they are qualified.

Tom and Mary may say no. In fact they may tell the most common lie retailers ever hear. It starts with a silly question.

A customer walks into a store and the retailer says" Can I help you?" The customer says, "No, I am just looking."

Crazy, and probably a lie. They are out shopping for the type of goods you sell in your store. If you wanted shoes you wouldn't be in an optician's, would you?

IMPORTANT RULE: Don't ask a question you don't mean, you may get an answer they don't mean.

PART THREE

BECOME A CLOSER

THERE IS NO SUBSTITUTE FOR AN EFFECTIVE PRESENTATION OR PITCH BUT SOONER OR LATER YOU ARE GOING TO HAVE TO CLOSE THE DEAL.
THE CLUE IS TO START CLOSING SOONER RATHER THAN LATER.
BE HONEST – ALWAYS TELL THE TRUTH

CHAPTER SEVEN

TWENTY CLOSES TO LEARN AND USE.

These are simple, short effective closes that anyone can learn, practice and use effectively. Work through them one at a time until you are comfortable. But first find a Practice Buddy. This is a great time to team up with someone who will act as your practice buddy and assist you to become well rehearsed and confident.

It can be a partner, friend or someone else who would like to become more 'sales accomplished', you can both learn together and that is fun.

After the first Close you're task is to find a Practice Buddy.

Just remember, a good presentation pre–handles all relevant objections. It can be as simple as an item, well displayed in a window or press advert. Your customer walks in and says, "I'll have it." That's great, the visual presentation did the work. The deal closed itself.

It may be you have a great website and people just sign up and buy through your online shop. That's great. Deal closed.

However, if you are the link then it is your verbal and visual presentation that has to do the job. Your presentations may lead to a simple "Yes" and that's great, but if it leads to questions or objections then don't be disappointed. It just demonstrates that your presentation almost did it, but now we need to actually close the deal.

Closing skills will not close a rubbish presentation or satisfy the need of a prospect who does not want whatever you are selling. If you have done everything you can then you can walk away, knowing just that; feeling good and looking forward to the next prospect.

Close #1 Ask for it

More sales are lost because the salesperson doesn't ask for the deal. In fact, I have watched some brilliant sales people talk themselves right into a wonderful deal, and then instead of asking for it and waiting for the answer – they keep talking, *and sell themselves the deal right back again!*

This is simple. Ask For It and then, SHUT UP and wait for the answer.

"So, Tom and Mary, will you be happy with this sofa in your home?" SHUT UP
Tom says "Yes" – deal closed. If he gives you a "No", with a reason then you can re qualify him.

Tom says "I think the back may be too high"

Re–Qualify

"So Tom – you are happy with the colour and shape and it's the right price for you, so it's just a question of the height of the back. Is that right?" Tom says "Yes." "Tom and Mary, can I ask you to show me a sofa that you prefer the height of? Tom says there isn't one.
"In that case Tom – this would seem to be the best choice for you if you want it in eight weeks time. Is that right?" You have just asked for it again - SHUT UP

Whoever speaks first is the buyer. You are the seller – stay that way! Keep quiet.

When you have asked a closing question, SHUT UP and listen to the answer.

TASK

Identify and talk to someone about becoming your Practice Buddy. Remember to tell the truth. Why have you identified this person? What makes them a great Practice Buddy?

It may go something like this:
" Hey Mike, can I ask you a favour? I have decided to become more effective in the way that I deal with people in my business life and I need a Practice Buddy to rehearse some mini phrases and presentations to. They are brief and quite fun too. Would you be my practice buddy?"

If Mike says "Yes," then that's great.

If he asks a question such as, "How long will it take?" or "What does that involve?" he is thinking of saying "Yes" and you will see that by using other closes, how simple it is to reach an agreement.

If Mike says "Why me?" you know why you selected him, so tell him the truth.

If Mike says "No" then move on to your next choice. Not everyone is going to say yes every time and that is a lesson worth learning.

YOU HAVE EFFECTIVELY USED CLOSE # 1

CLOSE # 2 THE ALTERNATE CHOICE.

Simply offer a choice. The selection confirms the deal.

"So Mary, do you want two three seater sofas, or a three and a two seater?"

Either choice means "Yes," it's a deal.

Never make the alternate choice a Yes or No, that would give a chance to stop the deal.

Let's have some fun.

You are at work or in a social setting and there is an attractive member of the opposite sex sitting with your crowd or in the same office. You would love to ask them on a date but are nervous they may say "No."

"Would you like to go out for a drink on Tuesday evening?" can lead to a No because they are genuinely busy on Tuesday or because it's a No anyway. So let's soften the close.

When the time is right, look them in the eye and say this.
" If I gave you the choice of a weekend in Paris or a weekend in Rome – where would you rather we go? Whichever place they choose – they have said yes to a weekend away.

YOU HAVE COMBINED TWO CLOSES. THE ALTERNATIVE CLOSE AND THE ASK FOR IT CLOSE, SO MAKE SURE YOU SHUT UP AND LISTEN FOR THE ANSWER.

NB. If they ask a question – they are interested in going. Keep at it because the temperature of this close is rising.

CLOSE # 3 THE MINOR POINT CLOSE

Not every closing question has to be definitive.

Sometimes small details will build confidence in both you and your prospect. Just use a question about a minor point to move the deal forward. Don't make it a major decision.

"Is the sofa going into a ground floor room?"
"Is there easy access to the room where the sofa will go?"
"Can we deliver any time of the day or is it just evenings / weekends?"
"Do you want cups with this to protect the carpet?"

After four minor questions like these, with positive answers, do you think they have decided to buy? Yes of course they have, in fact it would be a real surprise if they suddenly became negative.

A positive answer is a deal. Just close it.

"Then come with me Tom and Mary and let's do the paperwork."

If they say "no", that's no problem, just look surprised (who wouldn't be?) and go back to the last point of agreement and continue with the sales process. They aren't ready *yet!*

THIS IS AN EASY CLOSE TO USE AT ANY TIME, THE EARLIER THE BETTER.

Close # 4 The Handshake

A handshake has always been a clear sign of agreement and many men in particular find it easier to shake hands than say yes.

It is also a natural reaction to shake someone's hand when it is offered. Try it with people you meet.

Keep a note of the different actions of people. When you meet some, extend your hand and they will do the same – the handshake follows. To others, don't extend the hand and you will rarely find that they take the initiative.

Then start to use it at the end of conversations which reach an agreement. It may be that you agree to have lunch next Tuesday, so when you part simply extend your hand ready for the handshake and say "So see you next Tuesday Fred." Fred will shake your hand as confirmation.

"So Tom, Mary - these are the sofas you like and dark leather is the colour you wanted and I can have this ready for a six week delivery." Extend your hand. "Do we have a deal Tom?" Leave the hand outstretched waiting for the shake, look into his eyes and SHUT UP. Let the hand do the talking.

THIS IS USED AS A FINAL CLOSE ONLY.

CLOSE # 5 THE PUPPY DOG CLOSE

This comes from exactly what it says. All puppies are adorable. Some will grow into massive dogs and may be a pain but right here and now at a few weeks old they are so lovely. One gets put into your arms and it naturally shows affection and licks you and whimpers – adorable. It becomes very hard to give the puppy back. You want it.

You can do the same by getting Tom and Mary to sit on the sofa, get them to imagine watching TV or listening to music, relaxing. Ask Tom where he would have his side table for his drink. Get him one and position it. Do the same for Mary. "Tom, Mary what is you favourite TV show?" Now get them to imagine they are watching it.

"You look really comfortable there. How does this compare to your old sofa?" Let them savour the moment. "Close your eyes Tom – doesn't that feel comfortable for a nap?" Go quiet and leave them for a while. Walk away a little. One will turn to the other and make a positive comment.

Deal time is here – **now Ask for It!**

You will just have experienced another very important part of selling, **The Buying Signal.**

These are tell tale signs that your prospect is warming towards buying your product or service. They may touch it as if they own it. They may talk about using it or maybe positioning it, even perhaps getting rid of something they already own in order to make room for it. Watch out for these 'give away' signs that your prospect is getting warmer and get used to responding to them.

WHAT IS A BUYING SIGNAL?

A buying signal is only an indicator and depending when it comes up and how strong it is, dictates how you respond.

For example, let's say you are selling your car. You have taken a couple for a test drive and now they are looking around it. They are examining the car.

Tom asks "Is that boot is big enough to get the buggy in?" This is a buying signal because he is checking final details.

You may prompt the question as a trial close. "Mary is the boot OK for you to get the buggy in easily?" Why not get her to try the buggy in the car. When it fits, (and he will probably put it in for her) and says; " Is that OK for you?"
That's a buying signal.

Be on the lookout for these the whole time. Be ready to move forward and even close right there and then if the buying signal is strong enough.

Weak:

Tom says "Do you like this one Mary?"
Keep quiet

Medium

Tom says to Mary
"Will this sofa fit along that wall by the patio door?"
Keep quiet

Strong

Tom says, "Is there a discount for cash?"
Close – "Are you going to pay by cash Tom?"
SHUT UP.

How can you tell when you are close to a deal?

Well you may find your prospect using buying signals. They may talk as though they already own and are using the product. They may ask you questions that show their interest.

Equally they may come up with what appears to be an objection, or when you ask for the deal, they may say “I’ll think about it.”

Understand this part and you are well on your way to Becoming a great closer.

Q “What is the difference between water and steam?”

Steam ……………....
99° almost boiling….

At 99° it is water

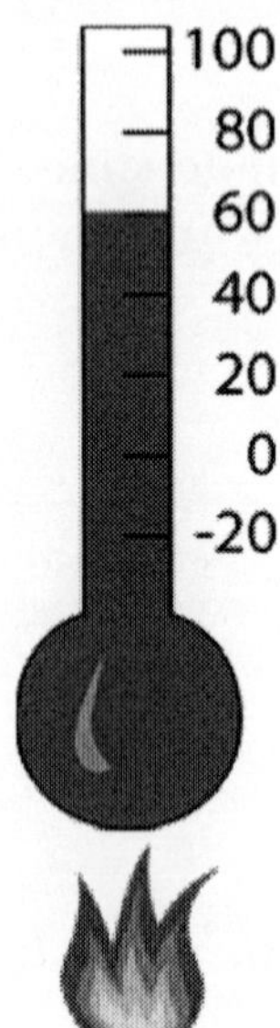

Water ………………

You are the flame

A. The difference is just one degree.
100 degrees = boiling point, the water turns to steam. Bingo!”
However at 99 degrees they often say, “I’ll think about it”

Keep going and boil the water.

When you begin any presentation your prospect is at best 'warm' and probably 'cold'.

You are the flame, applying enough heat to raise the temperature but not to crack the glass.

Not an aggressive flame that burns so intensely that everyone shies away, but a warm, welcoming flame. People with a need, gravitate towards you and that means not only a sale but an ever increasing supply of prospects who love doing business with you.

If you were to ask for the deal the moment you met your prospect the answer would almost certainly be No, unless pre selling had taken place, e.g. an advert led them to you.

If your prospect shows strong buying signals they are at boiling point and the water is turning to steam Close now. If you carry on the water may boil dry and there will no longer be any steam. The deal evaporates.

When you hear the words "I'll think about it," then they are at 99 degrees, almost at boiling point. Don't walk away now, the temperature will drop and you will never get as long to reheat it once they go cold. Stay with it and the flame will get them hotter and turn water into steam. Uncertainty to "Yes."

You can boil a gallon of water with a candle if you wait long enough. Be patient and stick with it. Have the next part of your presentation ready. That involves some subtle closing.

The next closes all follow an objection or reluctance demonstrated by your prospect. They are so interesting and such fun to use. Learn and enjoy them.

CLOSE # 6 THE WINSTON CHURCHILL

This one is a personal favourite of mine.

It is said that whenever he had a difficult decision to make Winston Churchill would take a sheet of paper and draw a line down the middle to form two columns. In the left hand column he would write all the advantages and positives about saying "Yes" and making the decision. In the right hand column he would write all the negatives. Whichever was the longer list would be his choice.

Do the same with your Tom and Mary.
You help them with the first list.

Positives	Negatives
You like the shape	
Its comfortable	
It will look great in your room	
It's a hard wearing material	
The cloth will keep looking good for a long time	
It's the colour you like.	
You can have it in the time frame you want	
It's within your budget	

Now leave them alone to complete the right hand column, they will struggle because you have them thinking about all the good points. After a few moments come back, look at the list and say, "Well, that seems to be very clear"

Now ask a closing question, "Did you want finance or are you paying cash Tom?"

Did Winston Churchill use this? I don't know but if he did, great, and if he didn't he should have!

Close # 7 Third Party Story

Tell them a story about someone else who had trouble deciding whether or not to buy their new sofa but finally made their choice and bought it. The day it was delivered their friends who always tried to be the 'top dog' and outdo everyone, came over for a drink and raved about their new acquisition and for the first time they felt like a million dollars.

The following morning they came back into the store and thanked me for helping them decide to buy – it was worth every penny to get that feeling and they loved the sofa.

This is designed to take buyers forward to the time when they take possession of their purchase. Who will see it first? Who will you want to contact and say it's arrived?

You see at this point in time of the sales process they may need to stop being concerned about the decision and focus on the benefit.

There has always been the famous story of Black and Decker who have sold millions of drill bits. When questioned how they sold so many, their owner said, "We don't sell ½ inch drill bits, we sell hundreds of ½ inch holes."

Get them to focus forward. No one has ever made a mistake in his or her future. All mistakes happened in the past.

Cautionary Tale

Similar to the Third Party Story, but told as a Cautionary tale and used as a salutary warning.

You may make it a negative story. For example, someone who went and bought a cheap sofa elsewhere and sixteen weeks later there was still no sign of it being delivered and the online company refuse to refund their money, saying it's on its way.

The moral, of course, is, "You only get what you pay for."

Now give them the positives from you.

"You know you wouldn't have that problem with us Tom, after all we are here for real, not just a page online."

Now close

"You want this in eight weeks Tom is that right?"

There is no risk in making a decision, the real risk is in either not making a positive decision because nothing in your life changes for the good, or making a decision to buy something 'on the cheap' and never being satisfied because you will always be comparing it to the real thing.

Task

Think about the product or service you sell and write down a positive and negative story that you could use. If you don't have one, speak to other more experienced people in your company and borrow a story from them.
The story should induce a warm glow by accepting, or fear and doubt about rejecting the deal. That is fear, not panic.

CLOSE # 8 CHANGE THE BASE

There are times when distance, time or cost, may become an objection. For example you are selling a telephone system and the client is 250 miles away from your offices.

They are concerned that if something goes wrong with their equipment, a local company would be more handily placed to deal with it and your company is too far away and so they will suffer higher call out charges or longer down time.

You cannot change the location of your company, but you can change the discussion to a challenge of time not distance.

You can explain that whilst the company is 250 miles away there is a local service engineer permanently based in this area and in fact you pride yourselves that you are normally on site within two hours of a call and very often even quicker.

By changing the base from distance to time you can handle it, and that works for any factor.

Perhaps change the down time factor.

"I agree our competition are only five miles away, but they will take your machine away for repair, we will either do it on site or leave a temporary replacement whilst we solve the problem. You will not be without a machine.
Service will resume as normal and that's important to your business, isn't it?"

CLOSE # 9 THE QUALITY CLOSE

Make sure you have presented the qualities of the product or service you are selling. Then reiterate that to your prospects.

"Tom, Mary – I don't know what budget you had in mind for your sofas, but can I assume from the detailed questions you asked that you want one which will look as good in a few years time as it does today?" Wait for the answer. Yes.

"In other words you want a good one, one that is well made with a good material covering it?" "Yes"

Well, we do have lesser quality and less expensive sofas but I don't think that is what you really want, is it?"

"This may be a bit more than you were thinking of spending but I think you agree that it has every quality you are looking for, am I right?"

"Can I ask you both, will you rather be happy knowing you chose the best quality or would you rather perhaps rue the choice you made when in a few years time, it is showing its age?" SHUT UP

Now you could have said "will you be happy knowing you chose the best quality?" and that will give you some indication of their feelings, but by adding, "Or would you rather perhaps rue the choice you made when in a few years time perhaps, it is showing its age?" That simple addition of the Alternate Choice Close makes this a much more effective closing question.

CLOSE # 10 THE ECONOMIC CLOSE

Price is always a factor for your prospects, and very often the article you are selling may be more than they had thought of spending. Let's keep going with the sofa analogy; it is several hundred pounds more than they originally had in mind.

The Economic Close uses the other factors surrounding the decision to put the price into perspective.

"Tom, the price is obviously more than you had thought to spend and it is of course your choice. Can I point out a couple of things though? You are redecorating that room. Did you do that cheaply, or well?" "I guess you could have bought cheaper decorating materials or a less expensive carpet, even cheaper curtains and light fittings, but judging by the attention to detail and care you are taking whilst buying this sofa, I know you are going to have a great room."

"Is it worth spoiling all that work by buying a cheaper sofa when you have taken so much care with the room and this is the one you really like?"

"You know this is not an £800 decision but part of a £2000 decision, isn't it?" (The total cost of the room).

"I am not being rude, but can you afford to buy this one?"
If Tom says "Yes," then Ask for it.(Close). If Tom says "No" then qualify him, "So if I can show you an easy way to spread the payment so that you can afford it, is it the one you want?"
SHUT UP

By adding Ask For It? It becomes a great closing sequence.

CLOSE # 11 COST V PRICE

There are always two figures that need to be considered when purchasing any product.

The Price is the amount you pay to own the item. The Cost is the amount you pay to use the item. Two very big differences.

Let's make it easy. A Printer cartridge is £50 to buy and closer investigation shows that it will print 5000 pages. A second brand is priced at £90 but when you check it out it delivers 15,000 pages. The first is priced at £50 but it costs 10p a copy to print. The second is priced at £90, but it costs 6p a copy to print.

The first is cheaper to buy but is actually more expensive.

You will always find a cheaper option than the product you are selling, you need to have a cost comparison to be able to use this close. Let's try with the sofa.

"Mary, these sofas are £900 and the others you have seen are only £650, and that's quite a difference."

There is always a reason for that but can I ask, "Would it be fair to say that the sofas we are seated on now are built to last? They have even been treated with a protective coating so that most stains or liquids can be wiped clean."

"I know the cheaper ones don't have that same quality."

"In addition, the stuffing in the cushions is made to last. In ten years time do you want to still be proud of your sofas or be forced to replace them because of their wear marks?"

"That would make the cheaper ones more expensive in the long run, wouldn't it?"

TASK

Work out five Cost v Price comparisons for your product or service.

It may reflect the life period of the product or production amounts. That may be the cost per unit produced.

It may be the life expectancy reflected in the guarantee. How does your guarantee compare to your competitor.
Decide the life expectancy and work out the cost per year.

These become prepared presentation routines so that you can call on them when you need them.
Preparation can be everything.
You will then have practised stories to use when you need to.

Salespeople are storytellers. Be prepared.

BE ON THEIR SIDE

When pitching, you should always be facing your prospects. You can then see their facial expressions and reactions. They can also see your face and particularly your eyes.
There comes a point however when you need to be 'on the same side' not on opposites. The next set of Closes should have the feel that you are working together to solve the challenge that will lead to a purchase. Try to be sitting side by side and in the middle of them if possible.
If you are writing, they can read it. You are now a team with a common aim – helping them make the right decision.

CLOSE #12
REDUCTION TO THE RIDICULOUS

This close takes some courage to use. It is specifically used when you are selling a top of the range item.

Let's imagine you are selling some upmarket, very expensive oven–to–table cookware, the kind that looks very smart and is guaranteed for life.

The drawback is that each pan is £100 as opposed to the cheap non–stick variety at £20 each or less. Mary wants the pans, the set of six cost £600 and Tom is dead set against the purchase but doesn't want to say so.

"Tom I know this sounds like an awful lot of money but let's just look at the next twenty five years of your happily married lives. These pans will keep going and going, they are made to look just as good then as they do now and Mary knows that older, broken–in pans cook the best don't they Mary?" Mary will agree – she wants them.

"These pans are £600, and over 25 years that is £24 a year or 50p a week. By eating just one home cooked meal a day, that's a cost of less than 10p a meal."

"Tom, where was the last place you went for a nice meal?" "Roughly how much did it cost?" "Was it absolutely perfect?" "And how much tip did you leave?" Let's say £5."

"So Tom, are you saying that you gave a waiter a £5 tip for an 'alright meal' that he didn't even cook, but it is too much to give your wife Mary a 10p tip every time she lovingly prepares your meal?"

NOW SHUT UP

CLOSE # 14 I'M PUZZLED?

This uses the Resume Formula but in a way that gets you to the heart of the real problem, which is normally, price.
Ask yourself, if the sofa you are selling was £10 then would we still be discussing it? Of course not. So let's get down to the nitty gritty.

List all the points, features and benefits they liked and then look puzzled.

"Tom, Mary looking back over all the points we have discussed and all the things that were important to you, we seem to have ticked all the boxes.

"Can I ask, what is it that is stopping us from going ahead with this?" SHUT UP

Many couples share all their finances today, but in many cases one will defer to the other when it comes down to the major financial decisions.

That person wants it; otherwise, they wouldn't still be here.

They are waiting for the one with the 'financial clout' to agree to the purchase. If you let them walk away now it is all over – the 'money' has won. Either the answer to this closing question will lead you to a deal, or lead you to which of the other closes you need to use in order to progress to a satisfactory conclusion. A deal!

This is a prime example of how closes can be used in sequence. You may often close the deal on the fourth or fifth time of asking. Don't be afraid to link Closes such as Minor Points followed by Alternate Choice and then Ask for I, then if needed use I'm Puzzled, then Ask for it again.

Be tenacious in a warm friendly way.

CLOSE # 15 SWAP SHOES

A very warm and friendly close, which in my experience of anyone selling an upmarket item, is totally applicable Imagine selling a home or a boat which you would love to own, that you are pitching to wealthy prospects. Show a pleasant envy of their ability to look at this level of purchase. and show how much you would love to be the owner.

"I would love to wake up every morning with a view like this from my bedroom window, it would make the start of every day feel great, wouldn't it?

"I wish my kids could have a big, safe garden this size to play in. I suppose you will be putting goal posts or climbing frames in will you?"

"I can only imagine what my friends would say if I invited them for a day on a boat like this. It certainly shows success, doesn't it?"

"I bet driving a car like this turns a few heads? It must be an amazing feeling. How long have you wanted one?"

Years ago I knew a blind estate agent who specialised in top–end homes in rural Hertfordshire. He had a driver to take him to the properties but once there would ask questions of the prospective buyers, making them his eyes.
"I am told this is a lovely sunny room, which has a great view. Does it? What can you see from here? Wow, that sounds wonderful."
He would continue in that vein showing pleasant envy of the homes they were viewing. At the end of each tour he would ask "Is the house as lovely as you have made it sound?" and "Would it make a great home for you and your family?" They sold it to themselves.
Let your prospect see what they want to see.

SWAP SHOES.

Close # 16 Ask for their help.

Again you need to have a puzzled look on your face and, if you have delivered a good sales presentation, you should be puzzled by now. Why aren't they saying "Yes" to your proposition?

This is very often tagged "The Last Ditch Close" because you genuinely want to know why they didn't buy.

Simply tell them that you feel you have let them down. This product would be ideal for them and yet, because you haven't done your job properly they are not buying it and you don't want to let your next customer down in the same way.

Let's examine this close more carefully.

The Close is designed to either close the deal or you can use it as a final qualification to let you do the same thing.
Go back through your sales pitch and examine each part.

"Did I fail to make you feel confident in my Company, Today Sofas, Tom?" The answer is "No," otherwise they wouldn't have continued any further than that point. This is simply to get them used to participating.
"Didn't you like the designs of the sofas we saw?" The answer is "Yes, we did," otherwise, they would have said so at the time.

Are you getting this yet?

"Was it the quality of build in our sofas?" Again "No."
"Are you still worried that we can deliver on time?" "No."

Then I am really stomped Tom, you and Mary seem to like everything about these sofas so why aren't you buying them?

NOW SHUT UP

It may be that you do find a point on which they are not entirely sold. This Close can identify the problem and turn it into an opportunity to close. Take another look.

"Did I fail to make you feel confident in my Company, Local Sofas, Tom?" The answer is "No," otherwise they wouldn't have looked any further than that point.
What if they "Yes." Then we can close.

First, use the objection as an opportunity to **QUALIFY.**

"Ok Tom, is there something that is bothering you?"

Your prospect now has to state the thing that is worrying them or the problem will wilt away. Just check though.

"Are you still worried that we can deliver on time?" "No."
Let's say the answer is "YES!" Either way turn this or any other point into a stone cold Close.

"Was it that you didn't you like the designs of the sofas we saw?" The answer is again "No," otherwise they would have said so at the time. If they say "Yes" we can deal with it and find one they do like, but there is another step first.

Use the objection as an opportunity to **QUALIFY.**

"Wasn't it the right quality of build in our sofas?" "No."
If "Yes" use the objection as an opportunity to **QUALIFY.**

"Oh I see. So Tom and Mary am I right in saying that you like the sofas, they are exactly what you want and you would be buying them now if you could be sure that you got delivery on time?" "YES"

This Close will either raise an objection, now you can qualify or it will make the objection disappear in which case;

CLOSE THE DEAL RIGHT NOW

QUALIFICATION SEQUENCE:

Let's continue with the same scenario.

"Oh I see. So Tom and Mary am I right in saying that you like the sofas, they are exactly what you want and you would be buying them now if you could be sure that you got delivery on time?" "YES" **Now Qualify**

"Tom, is that the only thing standing between us and a deal right now"

"Yes"

"And if I could satisfy you beyond any shadow of a doubt that delivery would be on time, would you order the sofas right now?" If they say yes we can deal with it and close.

If they say NO then your answer has to be, "So Tom can I ask what the real problem is?" and look puzzled, because you should be based on their previous answers.

You guessed it – The Price – it always comes down to money.

Now you revert to a Quality Close, or Price v Cost or any of the other closes that put you back in the deal.

You start making your reward when your prospect says No.

It simply means that you need to be prepared to deal with whatever objection comes at you and preferably by delivering a powerful sales presentation that made them want the deal and allows the 'heart rule to the head'. Then they just want the deal. If not, then the sequence of Objection – Qualification means you can close very comfortably.

CLOSE # 17 ROLE REVERSAL

Your prospect won't commit to the deal and yet has no specific reason. They are scared to say "Yes."

Reverse your positions.

"Tom and Mary, I am really at a loss here." (Just like the I'm Puzzled Close~ revisit the pitch.)

"Tom, Mary looking back over all the points we have discussed and all the things that were important to you, we seem to have ticked all the boxes, yet you are not saying "Yes I want them."
"Tom, what would I have to do to get you to buy these sofas?"

By asking them to answer that question, you put them firmly in the frame. One of two things will happen. They will either change their mind and say "Yes" to the deal, having discussed it between them or they will come out with a reason or an objection, then you can re – qualify ready to handle it and close the deal.

This is rarely the final close, but more than likely highlights their objections and allows you to clear the way for a sequenced close.

QUALIFICATION:
"
Tom, is that the only thing standing between us and a deal right now?" "Yes."

You know what to do now. **CLOSE THE DEAL.**

TASK

Choose three of the Closes we have discussed so far and explain them to your Practice Buddy.

Demonstrate their use.

Then try linking two together as a final closing sequence. For example; You have already done the presentation now, use The Winston Churchill Close followed by the Alternate Choice. Link them together.

Do this face to face rather than on the telephone and remember to sit alongside the person you are closing. Your attitude now has to be that you both want the same thing, so by moving from being on opposite sides of the discussion to where you are both on the same side, you can start to talk about "we need to solve this don't we Tom"

Ideally your practice buddy is also reading this book and can help you if you are floundering at all. Don't be scared to pick up the book and refer back.

Do this until, like an actor, you are 'off the book' and know your lines off by heart. Then you can deliver a real performance, a performance with emotion and power.

CLOSE # 18 The Take Away Close

Fear of loss is one of the prime motivation factors that govern decision making, especially when purchasing.

Using this close requires that you are practised and confident with it, otherwise you will simply look weak and stupid.

There are different means to effect the close. For example;

"Tom, I don't know if you were thinking of taking advantage of our no interest finance offer, but in these times the company only accepts first class applications. So before we talk about sofas, can I suggest we run an application past the scoring system so that I don't waste your time, only I have had three people turned down in the past few days. Do you have any bad credit history Tom?"

Most people will happily fulfil the credit check to prove how credit worthy they are, or will pull out a credit card as means of payment, saying that they have no problem affording any sofa you have in the store. That's exactly what you want to hear. Now you can use any close knowing that they can never say "I can't afford it" and mean it.

For example, now would be a great time to use the Quality Close. After all, they can afford the best.

.You could double check by using the Economic Close or go to the emotional Puppy Dog Close. Note how they start to dovetail and work in synergy.

FEAR OF LOSS IS A POWERFUL EMOTION – USE IT

CLOSE # 19 THE LIMITED OFFER

This is simple to use and yet one of the most effective closes of all. It again uses the powerful emotion, 'Fear of Loss.'

Let's look at two different examples to illustrate this.

Example 1

You are selling in a shop and there is a sale which ends today. Your prospects are having a tough time making their minds up. They want to think about it.

"Tom, you know that this sale ends today? You can say yes now at the sale price of £699 or come back tomorrow or in a few days time at the full price of £950. That would be crazy wouldn't it? **SHUT UP**

Example 2

You are selling face to face and they enquire about a product that was in the sale last week. The sale is now over.

Your customer says, "Can I still get this at the sale price?"

The amateur gives an answer "Yes" or "No."

The Closer Qualifies them and says "Is this the sofa you both want then?" "Yes."

Good tip: Amateurs tell, Professional Closers Ask.
If you want to learn something ask a question.

"So if I can get this for you at the sale price ~ and I don't know if I can, will you be buying this right now?"

If you can, the deal is there, if you cannot (I doubt that) then don't just say No, squeeze. They have already said they want the sofa. Now they do not want to lose it.

Go and ask a higher authority, your manager perhaps.

"Sorry Tom but the answer is No, partly because there are other people coming in to see it who know the sale is over – and by the sounds of it, they may well buy. However, the manager has said that he will waive the delivery charge if you want to buy it."

"Do you want me to put a sold sticker with your name on it?"

Don't just give information. Take the opportunity to qualify and ask a closing question whenever you can.

Start closing sooner rather than later.

When using 'Fear of Loss' you must be sure that they would like to own it and you must also deliver the question positively, with confidence and then **SHUT UP**

CLOSE # 20 ASSUMPTIVE CLOSE

I believe this is the most powerful of all the closes we have discussed because it uses your belief of how they are feeling to close the deal. You simply assume from the beginning that you are going to reach a deal. The challenge you have is to never put this in doubt. So many people, particularly retail shop staff, do exactly that. We want to deal in the truth and be honest and equally as important is that you keep your prospect honest.

Let's revisit the biggest mistake retailers make. Their prospect walks into the shop and they say: "Can I help you?" and their prospect replies as a reflex action, "No thanks, I am just looking."

Imagine everyone told the truth. A customer walks into a store, the retailer says" Can I help you?" The customer says "I don't know. Judging by the staff I have met so far – I doubt it ~ but we can give it a go if you want." Not the best way to start a relationship. Be warm, be polite but most of all be professional. Imagine being greeted with a cheerful "Good morning, how can I help you today?" Today is a great word– it means you are already asking closing questions.

They will now describe what they are looking for and the sale has started. From now on in, assume that you will conclude a sale and do everything with that positive thought in mind.

Ask 'assumptive questions'. "What time frame do we have to deliver your sofas?" "What colour have you decided on?" "Will you be wanting us to dispose of your old sofa?"

This is so easy. It puts and keeps them in the buying frame of mind, and people love to buy things they want.

It is an Assumptive Close because you naturally assume they want to buy and would be genuinely surprised if they didn't.

CHECKLIST AND TASK TIME

So here are the twenty closes. If you want to really make a difference to your results then you need to know all of these off by heart and understand how to use them.

Begin working down the list with your Practice Buddy,. Explain and demonstrate each one, until you are certain you know them. Then you can start to use them to close deals.

1. Ask for It
2. Alternate Close
3. Minor points
4. Handshake
5. Puppy Dog
6. The Winston Churchill
7. Third Party Story / Cautionary Tale
8. Change the Base
9. The Quality Close
10. The Economic Close
11. Cost v Price
12. Reduction to the Ridiculous
13. The Resume
14. I'm Puzzled?
15. Swap Shoes
16. Ask for their Help
17. Role Reversal
18. The Take Away Close
19. Limited Offer
20. The Assumptive Close

Once you are comfortable with all these closes, you can move on to the next two vitally important areas.

Part Four

Handling Objections Like a Pro'

THEY WONT ALWAYS JUST SAY YES.
WHEN THEY SAY "NO" IS WHEN YOU START
TO EARN YOUR COMMISSION

THE OBJECTION IS YOUR FRIEND.
IT TELLS YOU HOW WARM YOUR PROSPECT
IS TO YOUR PROPOSITION AND SHOWS
WHAT YOU HAVE LEFT TO DO. IT SETS YOU
UP TO CLOSE THE DEAL.

CHAPTER EIGHT

HANDLING OBJECTIONS

Up to now we have concentrated on closing presentations, and you will have noticed that many thrive on an objection from your prospect in order to be used effectively.

Closing questions solicit answers. Don't be fooled though. A "No" with a reason is not a hurdle but a springboard towards closing the deal.

For example you ask your prospect to go ahead and they say no because (A reason = the Objection)

Well the great news is that by the end of this section you will be fully equipped to turn that "No" into a solid "Yes," and it's all because they gave you an objection.

TASK

Before we start on objections, I want you to list the Top Ten reasons why people will tell you that you are not getting the deal you are pitching.

Then when you have finished this section you will test our formula on every one of them and realise that the world is about to become a very different place for you.

SO, WHAT EXACTLY IS AN OBJECTION?

Amateurs do things purely for the fun of it. Professionals do things for rewards. If you are looking to 'get paid' for closing the deal then you need to be and act like a professional.

To an amateur, Objections are the customer giving reasons not to buy, and they become intimidated as soon as they arise.

To the professional it is any question or statement which, when correctly handled gives you the opportunity to ask a closing question. If the customer had no interest they would say "No" so an objection actually shows interest.

So objections are 'friend not foe'. Most people treat objections as foes but you are now starting to understand what a vital part of your sales sequence they are.

They also denote the temperature of the sale at that time. You remember the thermometer

Boiling Point = Steam

The area of Objections

Water ....

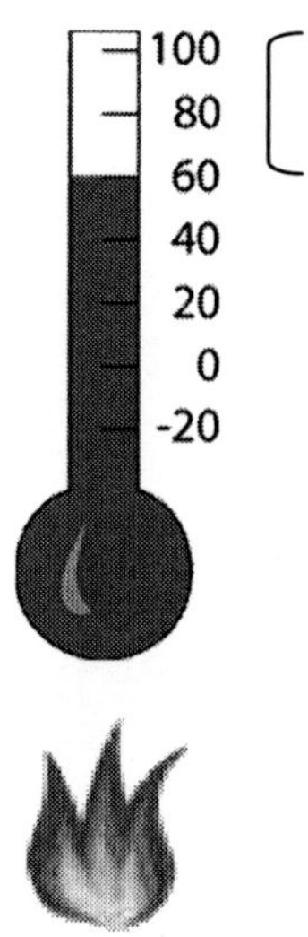

You are the flame

The water turns to steam at 100 degrees.

That's Boiling Point and equals "Yes it's a Deal."

Think about the thermometer in sales terms. Remember, at the very beginning of this sales conversation, your prospect was very cold and the mercury was way down the tube.

Your presentation became the warming flame pushing the mercury towards boiling point.

If you had asked a closing question such as Ask For It, at the moment you began, the answer would have been a stone cold "No." They were still too cold.
As they got warmer things began to change.
At sixty degrees, it was still a No
At over seventy degrees it's a No or a maybe. Objection time.

At ninety nine degrees it becomes "I'll think about it"

This is a major buying signal to a professional and very often a death sentence to the amateur.

"I'll think about it" is not an objection and you will see that if you try to treat it as one then your sale very often falls apart.

Why?

Because the moment you start to deal with it you give it 'life', your prospect repeats it with even more conviction and they convince themselves that they really aren't ready to buy.

I am about to give you a solid sequence that once learned and used in *exactly* the sequence I show you, will give you more success than any other method I have ever come across. Are you ready to really pep up your results?

CHAPTER NINE

OBJECTIONS – TRUE OR FALSE?

Sincere or insincere is a more accurate way of stating it.

When someone raises an objection, how do you know if they mean it or it is frivolous? Are they simply saying it to try and stop you closing the deal? Do they really mean it?

Use this step by step process and you will be amazed at the way objections either disappear because they were not important or real, or they become an opportunity to ask a closing question.

So here are the steps, learn them off by heart.

STEP 1 RAISE THE OBJECTION

STEP 2 IGNORE IT OR AGREE WITH IT

STEP 3 THEY REPEAT IT (IT MAY HAVE JUST DISAPPEARED)

STEP 4 YOU REPEAT IT BACK TO THEM IN THE FORM OF A QUESTION, CHANGING THE BASE.

STEP 5 QUALIFY IT

STEP 6 HANDLE THE OBJECTION EN ROUTE TO A CLOSE.

Let's take this step by step with an example.

Tom and Mary are our prospects, shopping for a sofa.

STEP 1 RAISE IT

You ask for the order. If they say "Yes" then great, if they say "No," then it normally takes the form of an objection. For example: Tom says "I am not sure about the cloth." Now I don't know if this is genuine or not, so let's find out.

STEP 2 IGNORE IT OR AGREE WITH IT.

"And you wanted a two seater and a three seater is that right Tom?" By being assertive, Tom may answer with their choice, in which case the original objection was insincere and disappeared. He may repeat it.

Agree with it. "So you like the style and shape of the sofas. Tom, did you want a two seater and a three seater or two three seaters?"

STEP 3 THEY REPEAT IT

"I am still not sure about the cloth." They only repeat it if it is genuine, if not is disappears.

This defines whether there is substance to the objection.

STEP 4 YOU REPEAT IT BACK TO THEM IN THE FORM OF A QUESTION, CHANGING THE BASE.

Repeat it back to them in the form of a question and at the same time change the statement to one you can handle.

"OK Tom, so if I understand you correctly, you like the sofa, it's comfortable and would look good in your room setting, but you are simply concerned that the cloth isn't hard wearing enough. Is that right?"

Tom agrees ~ it sounds genuine.

STEP 5 QUALIFY IT

"And is that your only concern Tom?"   "Yes."

"OK Tom, if I can satisfy you that this sofa will last the way you want it to, can we close on this right now?"

If they say "Yes," then let's handle it.

If they say "No," they will give another reason and we still need to requalify. Remember he said this was the only concern and now he is changing his mind.

Notice how we have changed the base, from 'hard wearing' to 'how long will it last'?

STEP 6 HANDLE THE OBJECTION EN ROUTE TO A CLOSE.

"Tom, I am so glad you liked this set and chose this particular cloth". Do you remember when we looked at the silk type finish. I said – "Great for show, but certainly not right for a family to use. It simply wouldn't last."

"The leather sofas you saw look better as they age providing they are like ours with good skins rather than the paper thin ones that are sold very cheaply. You do only get what you pay for don't you?"

"And I have to say Tom and Mary, that you have certainly chosen a warm comfortable cloth and by opting for the stain resistant finish you can look forward to getting many many years service and it will still look good."

"There is one other advantage to the sofa you have chosen. Because they have loose back and seat cushions. In ten or twelve years time you can have them restuffed very easily and go back to the shape they are today. So the life of these sofas is really just determined by when you get fed up with them, and then I bet someone you know will be glad of them and get even more use out of them and be delighted."

Now Close it

"And you do like the colour and look of them don't you?"

You see the objection handled properly has led to a closing question – it was your friend not your foe.

Objections are a great part of your success tools, learn to use them as friends.

Make sure you don't fall into the amateur trap.

What do I mean by the 'amateur trap'?

Well let's revisit that objection.

You ask for the order. They say "No," and it is normally in the form of an objection.

For example: Tom says "I am not sure about the cloth"

The wrong way of trying to move forward is to question it there and then.

You ask Tom, "What is it about the cloth you don't like Tom?" He now reinforces his point with colour or wear factor or something else, but this is now starting to become a major issue to him when it may well have been an insincere objection and disappeared of its own accord. Now it is real. You have just lost control of the deal

This applies in everyday life too. There are times when you are dealing with things that crop up such as your teenage son or daughter is going out for the evening and you give them a time to be in by. They violently object to the time set – let's say 11pm. If you go at this head on, then the conversation will degenerate as they dig their heels in.

Let's use the principle in a non selling scenario.

STEP 1 RAISE IT

"And Tom, I want you home by 11pm."

Tom says, "Dad that is ridiculous, it's way too early"

STEP 2 IGNORE IT OR AGREE WITH IT

"And how are you getting home from the party?"

STEP 3 TOM REPEATS IT

"Well I would share a taxi, but 11pm is far too early for the others to leave."

STEP 4 YOU REPEAT IT TURNING IT INTO A QUESTION.

"So Tom, are you saying the problem is that if you have to leave before 11pm then no one else will be going that early and you wouldn't be able to share a taxi?"
"Yes"

STEP 5 QUALIFY IT?

"Is that the only issue Tom, being able to share the cost of the taxi?" If Tom says yes, then you could if you wish, find out the cost of the cab and share that cost in order to get him home by 11pm.
If Tom now says, "No, the problem is that I don't want to leave that early," then continue with the process.

STEP 4 YOU REPEAT IT TURNING IT INTO A QUESTION.

"OK Tom, so what time did you have in mind?"
Tom knows you were aiming for 11pm so he is unlikely to say 2am. His reply to you is either an opportunity to negotiate and close, or you treat it as a further objection.

Tom says "Midnight"

STEP 6 HANDLE THE OBJECTION ON THE WAY TO A CLOSE

And you will definitely be here by midnight?"

Closed and both parties are happy. As I told you right at the start, that is important.

What if Tom says 2am and that doesn't suit you? Now treat it as another objection. Now back track to **STEP 4**

STEP 4 YOU REPEAT IT TURNING IT INTO A QUESTION.

"Tom do you honestly think that 2am is a reasonable time?"
"Do you really expect me to agree with that?"
Your agreement is now the question.
Tom says, "Well I guess not"

Step 5 Qualify it?

"Tom, I want you to have good time so let's not fall out. What time would we have to say for us both to be happy?"

Tom's answer becomes the easier route to a close. We know it will be between 11pm and 2am, it is now a question of negotiation and therefore a close.

Tom answers and depending on how you feel about the time, you either repeat the process or close

Step 6 Handle the objection and close.

"OK Tom so here is your choice, you can either be home for midnight and I will split the taxi fare with you or you can be home for 1am and you pay. Which do you want?"

You see closing is something that goes on in everyday life. It becomes a structured way of handling conversations that have an outcome that you wish to influence. Done softly, and with a quiet confidence this will make life so much easier and more fruitful.

If you don't have an end goal in mind then two things happen. Firstly you cannot possibly get the result you want because you have no clear idea what that is, in which case the second thing happens – the other person gets the result they wanted and that may leave you feeling frustrated.

Remember, every time you enter this process, a close will take place and either they buy what you have to offer or you buy their reason for saying no. It is your choice.

CHAPTER TEN

I'LL THINK ABOUT IT

Now is the time to realise why this is not an objection.

Lets go back to the thermometer.

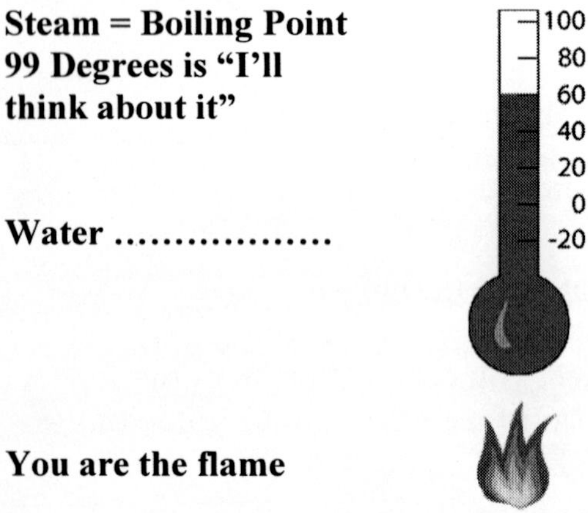

At 99 degrees the water still has not yet turned to steam – almost but not quite. When you first started the temperature was cold and had you tried to close the answer would almost certainly have been NO.

As you were delivering an effective presentation so the temperature started to rise, it is almost at boiling point. You try to close and your customer says "I'll think about it"

If you allow the conversation to end here, then the flame (you) has been removed and the temperature will drop. That means it moves away from boiling point and the water cools. You will never be allowed the same 'heating time' again and the deal will slip away.

Notice I didn't say it was lost.

You cannot lose something you don't have yet!

Realise that your customer is now very close to a yes and find out what extra heat you need to apply in order to turn the answer into a YES and close the deal.

It is very similar to handling an objection but not quite. You don't ignore it – far from it.

Be enthusiastic and say "I am delighted that this is something you are now thinking about doing, and I am sure we can tie up the loose ends so that you will be happy with the deal. Tell me, what we need to do to get this right for you and we can tie the whole thing up.

Either they will tell you and you can close or they will switch to another objection and you know how to handle that.

I'll think about it is a great place to be if you know what you are doing – and now, YOU DO!

TASK

Sit down with your Practice Buddy and use this imaginary scenario to rehearse your closing techniques.

You are selling office desks and chairs.
Your Practice Buddy is looking to refurbish his home office and wants a new desk and chair. He is interested in the light oak pedestal six drawer locking desk and the brown leather chair . It is £550 and has a lower priced alternative with four drawers locking at £450 or not locking at £400. Delivery is normally four weeks but you have them ex stock.

Try to close a deal using at least two closes and Handling any objections that may arise.

You can do this, now prove it to yourself.

By the way – show this page to your Buddy and make them understand that they are there to help by playing the interested customer's role, not to just say "No, No, No," as that isn't helping you.

Get comfortable one step at a time and go through the scenario using different closes and different genuine objections. Make it fun and you can learn to enjoy it.

Kick off with this sequence.

Alternate choice followed by
Minor Point followed by Ask for It.

The Objection is "I really don't want to spend that much."

PART FIVE

HANDLING OBJECTIONS

THERE WILL ALWAYS BE THOSE TIMES WHEN YOUR CUSTOMERS JUST WONT SAY YES. THEY PUT UP OBJECTIONS AS REASONS NOT TO DECIDE RIGHT NOW.

WHY NOT LET THEM BECOME YOUR BEST TOOLS IN CLOSING THE DEAL?

CHAPTER ELEVEN

PRE HANDLING OBJECTIONS

There are two distinct ways of handling objections. The first is the method we have discussed so far which is to Raise it and then go through the process for handling them.

The second is to pre–handle the objections by including them in your presentation, thereby removing them as you present.

If you examine all the sales presentations you make for your company, product or service, there are genuine points that come up time and time again and if they weren't covered would almost certainly come up at the end. For example

"What guarantee do you offer?"

"What back up service is there if anything goes wrong?"

"I have never heard of you, how do I know you are genuine?"

There are many more and they are easily dealt with by using a structured, planned presentation.

This does however leave one possible challenge. Many people feel they ought to have an objection or two at the end. They often feel 'buyer's reluctance' and in the same way that they walk into a shop and say "I am just looking" they feel they need to raise an objection.

Well here is a million dollar question.

How would you like to only get one objection at the end of your presentation, and best of all it is the one YOU choose?

This is a simple skill that once mastered makes life so simple and coupled with a well delivered sales pitch really works.

YOU PICK THE OBJECTION

Think about presentations or pitches you have done to date. There are a number of objections that you may have heard. Often it depends on the value and type of product you are selling. For example if you are direct selling home improvement products with a high value then the source finance may well be an objection. For example "I will need to talk with my bank to see what a loan would cost me."

If you allowed the conversation to stop there then a sale cannot take place so you need to be able to handle it.

It may be about a car and the young person you are talking with needs to find out what the insurance quote would be before they can decide to purchase. The same thing applies.

With our example of buying a sofa, it maybe that they say they need to check the size of the room before they say "Yes."

You can no doubt identify the most common objections you come across and the way to make life so easy for you, is by you knowing how to pre–handle them before they arise.

TASK

List the five most common objections you encounter.

1

2

3

4

5

Pre -Handling Objections (cont)

Check your presentation or pitch. Does it cover the objection you don't want to hear?

For example:

They need to check the room size.

During your presentation you would ask the size of the room and pre qualify that you will only show them sofas that would fit their setting. It would be a good idea to have some graph paper and draw the room with doorways and chimney breasts etc.

By covering this point and pre qualifying the size, then it cannot come up at the end as an objection.

Make a list of all the things that you face again and again and pre handle them by including them in the pitch.

Now if you do that with every possible objection, something so ridiculous will happen that it defies belief and becomes almost impossible to deal with because it is such a lie.

So the idea is to now only leave one not covered during the pitch, but actually get them to bring it up and let them have it. Then at the end you can remind them of their objection and they will use it if they want to delay their decision. As it is the one you have chosen because you can handle it, then you will be home and dry. The only problem you may face is boredom from continually dealing with "Yes" to the deal or the same objection all the time.

Let's see how it works.

Tom and Mary are looking for a sofa. During your preliminary discussions you have decided the size, number of units and seats etc. and the time frame for delivery.
You are about to begin looking at sofas and you bring up the subject of payment.

"Tom, can I ask whether you have considered how to pay for this purchase or were you going to see the price of the sofas you like and then approach your bank to see their rates for a loan?"

Tom say "Yes I am," it leaves him a nice way out.

You go ahead and look at the ranges available and Tom and Mary choose their sofa, but they are reluctant to seem enthusiastic about their decision.

Instead of simply going for a close by Asking For It, you qualify the close including the objection you want.

RAISE IT

"So Tom and Mary, it looks like you have made your choice. Apart from wanting to discuss the finance with your Bank Manager is there anything else that would stop us going ahead with your order?"

They will either say "No lets go ahead, that is the one we want," or they will take the escape route and say, "No I just need to talk with the Bank before I do."

INSTEAD OF IGNORING IT – AGREE WITH IT

"Great so you have decided that is the one you want it is now just a question of who can lend you the money at the best rate. Is that right?"

"Yes, we will talk with the bank and then when they say yes we can order the sofa from you"

QUALIFY IT

"Tom, if I can guarantee you the cheapest loan available to you even if that is your banks' would you want it?"
The answer has to be yes.

HANDLE IT EN ROUTE TO A CLOSE

"Well Tom all we have to do is get you pre-approved by our finance facility with a guaranteed rate, which you don't accept right now. Then you can go to your bank knowing you have one loan approved and it is not a question of will they lend you the money, but can they beat our rate.
Perfect isn't it?"

CLOSE

"OK Tom let's get you a pre-approval and then on the day of delivery you can decide which is the best loan to take. OK?"

You could just as easily use delivery time as the objection you want.

During the presentation you purposely don't discuss the delivery time they require. You get them to mention it but don't cover it. Let's say they mention six weeks.

You go through the process of choosing a sofa and they are non–committal about their choice. You feel that by simply asking for the order you will get an excuse or objection as a reason not to buy, so you use the same planned objection route.

"So Tom it looks like you have made your choice and chosen this sofa. There is only one problem and that is delivery. I don't think we can do this one in the six week time frame you want. Is that a real stumbling block?"

If Tom says "No" then you have a deal.

If Tom says "How long will it be," then he wants the sofa.

If Tom says "That makes it a NO," then we have the answer. Provided of course that you can deliver.

This is an important part of the pitch – you have to be able to fulfil their requirements. Always tell the truth.

Fulfilling their order and getting paid are the two most important factors in any deal, so you must be truthful otherwise there is no point in getting their agreement.

CHAPTER TWELVE

QUALIFYING YOUR PROSPECT

There are criteria that need to be in place before you can confidently deliver a presentation which would result in you closing the deal. If the criteria are not available then you should warm up the situation with courteous information that, at the same time, will allow you to qualify your next meeting. Never pitch unless you have a qualified prospect.

Good qualification points are:

Are all parties to the decision present?

If you are not talking to all the decision makers then the likely outcome is that they will consult and get back to you.

Are there any outside factors that affect the decision?

If you are selling a kitchen and the extension plans are yet to be agreed then you cannot get a final close. You may however, by further discussion be able to close "subject to the extension being approved by the local authority" etc.

You can of course be direct and simply ask "are you looking to buy your ……… today ? Do not add "or are you simply browsing?" because that is the same as a retailer asking "Can I help you?" and we know that invites the lie of "No, I am just looking."

Build your own criteria list so that you can qualify your prospects without turning it into an interrogation process but ensure that you are able to close the deal today.

CONDITIONS

There are conditions that may exist under which the best salesperson in the world could not close the deal. It would be pointless to battle these conditions and then think that your presentation skills are at fault.

By conditions I mean for example your prospect has no need for your product or service. (You are selling pet insurance and they don't have any pets.)

You cannot fulfil their criteria. (They want a sofa delivered today and all of your items are a fourteen week delivery and there are none which are ex stock.)

They have absolutely no means to pay and due to their credit rating you cannot offer them any finance facilities.

They are dead! That may sound extreme but you may be hard pushed to find another genuine condition which would stop the best salesperson in the world closing this deal.

By condition I don't mean an objection that they bring up at the very beginning and want you to accept that as a reason you could not close right here and now.

For example, you are visiting someone in their home to sell a new kitchen and they tell you right up front that they are getting three quotes and you are the first. Some sales people would choose to come back another day when they would be the third to quote thereby treating this as a condition.

IT IS AN OBJECTION NOT A CONDITION.

Ask yourself, if you design a kitchen that they absolutely love and it falls within their expected price range do you think it is possible they may say "hey we don't need to look elsewhere, this is the one for us?"

If you leave now, one of the other companies may be good enough to do exactly that and you won't even get a chance to pitch these prospects.

That also means if you do a great job, you would be the last salesperson in there and no one else got the chance to pitch.

Later, I will share some real closing sequences with you which will illustrate exactly how to close effectively and you can of course adapt them to your own business.

Treat it like any other objection either ignore it or agree with it. You may decide to repeat it turning it into a question that you can handle. For example; "and I guess if none of those three quotes suited you, then you would keep looking, is that right?" "So Tom quite sensibly you are not necessarily going to take the first, second or third quote, you will only order a kitchen when it is exactly what you want at the price you are prepared to pay. Is that right?"

Now don't fall into the trap of trying to close by saying "so if I showed you a kitchen that you really love at a price you want to pay then we could go ahead today?" because they will feel backed into a corner and you will alienate yourself. Save it for later.

Deliver your full presentation and build desire and confidence within them. When you are absolutely sure that your design has ticked all their boxes, then you can move on to working out a price.

Now look at how the outcome can change depending on the skill of the closer.

Non skilled amateur

Works out a price and then delivers it.

The prospects say "Thank you very much we will get back to you when we have the other quotes." It's very hard to come back from there because they said it up front and have now repeated it. More importantly, you feel despondent.

Semi skilled.

Works out a price and then tries to be clever. "I know you said that it depends on how much it is, what price do you think a kitchen like this will cost?" That is so trite.

Would you honestly expect them to tell the truth? Would you? No of course not. You would say less than you expected and so will they. You now are going to proceed on the back of a lie. Very hard to stop any further lies now.

The skilled professional.

Having completed the design and seen their delighted response, the professional qualifies his prospect.

"Can I ask you Tom, if you had come to buy this house and this was the kitchen that was here, would you be over the moon with it and would you have bought the house and kept the kitchen?" They answer yes. After all they did buy the house and they say they love the kitchen.

RAISE IT

"Can I ask you Tom, Mary, if this kitchen comes within your budget would there be any reason to look any farther?"

IGNORE IT

He delivers the price and then judges their reaction. If it is favourable he qualifies again by asking a closing question.

"So, you now have a kitchen design that you love at the price you are prepared to pay, why don't we do the paperwork and get it underway?"

Depending on the answer you either have a deal right now or an objection.

THEY REPEAT IT

"No we did say that we are going to get three quotes and we still want to do that."

YOU REPEAT IT TURNING IT INTO A QUESTION.

"I understand Tom, just let me make sure I have it right. You love this kitchen and it's everything you want. The price is within your budget and you just want to make sure you are doing the right thing. Is that right?" "Yes"

"Can I ask you both, if you had already seen the other quotes and mine was slightly less or more expensive would we be going ahead right now? A qualified yes, they will never just agree unreservedly.

Now is when the Closer goes to work and earns their commission.

For example –

"I know when we first sat down you told me you would get three quotes and I respect that." However can I ask you, "What would another quote have to deliver, for you to not want to order this kitchen?" Notice I didn't say "Choose their kitchen." Never speak about your competition positively.

The reply is either that the design would offer something more but they have already agreed this is perfect. Or, The price for a similar kitchen would have to be cheaper and you can close on that or they are simply sticking to their guns.

Be forthright and honest.

"Tom, I really want to do this deal with you because I know we can do a good job, you will be happy and that can lead to further work by referral and that is so important to me."

"I know my competition and what they have to offer. Can I ask who else you have booked to see you?"

If they cannot name the other companies this was definitely just an objection without substance. If they can name them then you simply move on.

Why not ask the obvious question. "What would I have to do to get you guys to say yes to me tonight?"

Choice 1 – They say "There is nothing you can do."
Choice 2 - They say "You would have to offer a deal or a discount on the price."

The amateur says "How much discount?"

The Pro will requalify. "So are you saying that if we could adjust the price sufficiently, you would place your order right now?"

The answer is either "Yes," or "No" with the same reason as before. If it's "Yes" then proceed.

"Well the price list is the price list. I cannot change that but what sort of difference would there need to be?"
Let's say the quote was £12,500 and Tom replies £11,000.

Now look what has happened. Beforehand you had to close a £12,500 deal. Now you only have to close a £1500 deal – the difference between the two prices. They have also shown they are able to make a £1500 decision, because they could manage to reply "£11,000."

Re Qualify with a close.

"So if we can get the price down to £11000, you will go ahead and order the kitchen is that right?" Unless they say "Yes" there is no point taking this next route.

"OK then what about if we put in a less expensive work top?" They don't want that.

"What about we fit less expensive appliances or leave out the wine cooler and the silent close doors?"

Keep reiterating the things that made them love the quality of this kitchen so much. They don't want to lower the spec.

NOW CLOSE.

"You know Tom and Mary, I could have come in here and only ever shown you the kitchen designed to a lower spec and you wouldn't have necessarily realised the difference,. Take the worktops for example. I could have shown you good quality tops instead of the very best we have available. Now you know you don't want that, do you?"

In today's economy every company has made sure its prices are competitive and to lower the price by any significant amount would mean lowering the quality. That's obvious isn't it?"

"So for another company to come in here and quote a lower price, something about the kitchen must be cheaper or to a lower spec and you have said you don't want that right?"

"Can I ask if you can afford this price level of kitchen?"

The answer is probably "not quite" but they are reluctant to admit that.

Here are some closes you can use.

"Guys can I ask how much you paid for your house?" £400k

"Then can I ask that having spent £400,000 pounds to get to this position it is crazy to spoil the whole thing for £1500 – wouldn't you agree?"

Or

"So you spent £400,000 on this great house but with a kitchen you wanted to rip out. You bought it knowing you would replace the kitchen. If the house had already been done with this new kitchen and they had asked £415,000 would you have walked away from the deal?"

If all that fails, then you can take a business decision. If you go away and then return on another occasion, we have already said you would be on 50% commission (two visits) so why not secure the deal now by splitting your commission. Tell them exactly why you are about to suggest that, but make it clear this is only good for tonight because you will not work for 25% of your original commission by splitting it and then taking two trips. You would rather go somewhere else on full commission.

You must then stick to your guns – it takes courage!

If they say, "You are not telling me that if I call you in a few days time, come back for our order that you will say No?"

Your reply should be "No, I will happily take your order, I want your business but it will be at the regular price, not less 50% of my commission because by coming back, I cannot be with another customer in a different home that night. My offer is a commercial business decision and I would ask that you respect that"

In order to be effective you must maintain your integrity. If you make a definite statement like this, then mean it. Don't back down. By all means negotiate but once you have made that definite statement stick with it. If you cannot do that, then do not say it in the first place.

Tell the truth.

If they then still maintain they want to get two more quotes, ask the final closing question.

"Tom, what price would we have to make this kitchen to secure your order tonight?"

If they answer that with a figure, then they are saying they would buy without two other quotes. The objection is a price based one, it is not about getting two other quotes.

You remember I said you have to keep both of you honest. Well now you have to make this an honest conversation without insulting your prospect.

"Tom, I cannot change the price list, but are you saying that there is a price at which you would place your order with me right now? If he says yes, then ask – "Tom, what would that price be?" Don't be scared – ASK!

Let's reinforce something here. Closing is no substitute for a well delivered effective presentation. However, if you have presented well and 'ticked all the boxes' then you are going to have to close sooner or later. It may not be the first close that works. It may take three, four or even more attempts.

Think of this equation. If you know more ways to get them to say yes (closes) than they have ways to say No (objections) then you will close more sales than ever before.

CHAPTER THIRTEEN

FEEL FELT FOUND

This is a another very simple way to handle any objection. It is gentle, harmonious and cannot disturb your prospect.

They make a statement or raise an objection about a specific point, normally a preconceived idea. Imagine you have experienced this before for yourself (and you probably have) then simply share how you felt until you found out that......

Your prospect says "I don't want to go on a cruise because 99% of the passengers are geriatric"

You respond,

"I know how you **FEEL**, that's exactly how I **FELT** until I **FOUND** that there are now ships who specialise in the under thirty five age range and all the entertainment is aimed at them, everything from Discos to Cinema films and the way the bar entertainment is planned."

Another example could be that they have seen sofas at a much lower price.

You can apply this formula to absolutely anything, so if you ever get stuck – this is a great escape route.

"I know how you **FEEL**, that's exactly how I **FELT** until I **FOUND** that the material wasn't flame retardant and the frame wasn't beech wood but compressed fibreboard. That just isn't the right quality is it?"

TASK

Work with your practice buddy using **FEEL FELT FOUND** until you are really comfortable with it.

HOW ABOUT THIS FOR A PROMISE?

"YOU NEVER NEED TO HAVE SOMEONE SAY NO TO YOU AGAIN."

Wow, how can I say that? Well it's simple.

GOLDEN RULE OF CLOSING

Never ask the final closing question unless you are sure the answer will be "Yes."

How do you do that?

You use a series of trial closes followed by intermediate closes until you know that your prospect is totally onside. Only then do you ask that final, closing question.

This is the time when you realise that closing is a process not an event. Just simply crashing in with a closing question will often lead to an absolute disaster, and that can kill the entire rapport you have built so far.

Some people find it very hard to commit to a decision. You may think they find it hard to say "Yes," but in fact they find it almost as difficult to say "No." I did say almost.

This next part lets you use a "No" as a "Yes" and after all they find it easier to say no, don't they?

Reverse Closing

Also called Negative Closing. This is a great tool to use with those people who have a really hard time saying "Yes." You simply ask the closing question in a way that when they say No they mean Yes.

For example.

Instead of asking "Do you want the marble worktops?" and getting the answer, "Well I am not sure,," you phrase it in the negative.

"Mary, you don't want laminated worktops do you?" the answer is "No" but that becomes a positive statement.

"Mary, you are not bothered about having your kitchen fitted before Christmas are you?" You want the answer of "Yes."

However, if you phrase it this way – "Mary, would a January fitting be OK?" No it would not (I want it before Christmas) the "No" is in fact a "Yes."

Reverse closing cannot be extensively used as the prospect will feel uncomfortable working in the negative, however when used sparingly it can start them making decisions and lead you towards your ultimate goal.

KEEP IT SIMPLE – A STORY

Children can see things so differently.
I was told about this by a man who was sitting in the bar when it took place.

My six year old son went down to the bar of a hotel we stayed in regularly, climbed onto the stool and asked the barman, "Can I have a Coca Cola with ice and lemon please, and can you charge it to room 6?"f
The barman was eighteen, and on his first ever shift. He was uncertain whether or not he could let such a young boy sign the chit. He therefore started a long monologue why he didn't think he could do that.

My son replied "Sorry, it was a drink I wanted not an argument."

The onlooker suggested that for fifty pence it was worth taking the risk.

Was he precocious? No.

My Son knew what he wanted, and was focussed on getting the drink he asked for.

That's Closing.

PART SIX

THE EMOTIONS OF A SALE

LET THE HEART RULE THE HEAD. THE HEART MAKES DECISIONS THROUGH EMOTION. THE HEAD TENDS TO ANALYSE AND ANALYSIS LEADS TO PARALYSIS.

MAKE THEM WANT TO ACT.

THE EMOTIONS BEHIND DECISIONS.

Emotions play the major role in decision making during a purchase. We buy through emotion not logic, in fact this is the time when the 'heart really does rule the head'.

There are four emotions that govern a sale and if you are going to be a professional, when it comes to closing, then you need to understand and embrace these powerful motivators.

LOVE

NEED

FEAR

GREED

And the catalyst that fires them all is

CURIOSITY

Curiosity will bring them all into play.

Watch a fish approaching the bait. It smells good, looks attractive and the fish is not quite sure, but in the end curiosity makes that fish strike for the bait and it is hooked.

Love, Need, Fear and Greed are the attractive bait that lure us all, but curiosity is the thing that gets the better of us and makes us 'bite.'

Do you remember the film Dirty Harry, where Clint Eastwood shoots the punk at the very start of the movie and then stands over him showing him his Colt 45 – the most powerful handgun. "Did I fire five times or six?" he asks, pointing the gun at the dying punk who says "I need to know." Curiosity makes sense of this crazy statement

Remember:

People do not buy through logic, they buy through emotion and the catalyst that evokes all four emotions is curiosity. In the sales role, your job is to invoke that emotional desire via one of these or all of these four avenues, and curiosity is the powerful emotional trigger to open the door.

Why are they so important? Why do they work?

Love

If you fall in love with something or someone then the heart will rule the head and you will, without hesitation make decisions you would perhaps not normally contemplate. It doesn't matter – you will do anything to get what you want. You are in love and that is that.

Need

If you have a burning desire and a need so great that it is all you can think about, then likewise you will do whatever it takes to get what you want.

Logic disappears, and the heart will rule the head.

Fear

Fear of loss is a powerful emotion. If you are scared and feel that you almost have something but it is slipping away from you, then you will again act irrationally, making decisions and acting in a way totally against your logical character and the heart will rule the head.

No one likes feeling they may lose something, especially when they have yet to own it. Prior to ownership, all things are perfect. They are so attractive, we don't want to lose out.

Greed

Greed is a powerful emotion. People who have, want more. Then they want more and more. They start to gather things towards them and if you present an opportunity to feed that greed, the heart will rule the head

This is not you trying to manipulate your customers. You are simply making sure that you allow their buying experience to be enjoyable, and by triggering their emotions, they lower their preconditioned buying defences and start enjoying themselves. Buying is fun!

That means you are now dealing with people that want to buy and own, not those that are scared to decide.

There is however a significant barrier to these triggers being fully activated and that is the issue of Trust.

TRUST

During your sales conversation and pitch, you must build trust in your prospects' minds. Unless they feel confident in you, your organisation, product or service, the emotional factors cannot come into play.

Reputation and Testimonials play a huge part in developing that trust. Make sure you gather letters and e–mail testimonials from your personal clients to support your presentation.

There is a great phrase "Documentation beats conversation" and when building that 'trust factor,' nothing could be more pertinent.

When you are closing, there will be times when you use confirmation of such details as delivery, payment, guarantees, quality of workmanship etc and unless your prospects trust you then they count for nothing.

It is almost impossible to gain that trust during the closing process, you must have built that strong base earlier in the sale.

I started by saying you have to deal in the truth. Truth links with trust and if you once betray that trust you cannot regain it, so make sure you stay truthful and ethical throughout your dealings otherwise your sales career will be a short one full of struggles.

Winston Churchill is reputed to have used a very simple but effective way to establish trust and at the same time carry the points he wanted to make.

As an orator he said everything in threes. Adolf Hitler and John F. Kennedy, Margaret Thatcher and Tony Blair all used the same tactic.

THE RULE OF THREE

People remember facts more easily if they are delivered in threes. The Rule of Three has been used since Aristotle. Just think of the famous quotes and commonly used terms.
As easy as A B C
Friends, Romans, Countrymen - Julius Caesar
Education, Education, Education – Tony Blair
The Good, the Bad and the Ugly – Film
A mars a day helps you **Work , Rest and Play**
Veni, Vidi, Vici – Julius Caesar
Spend Spend Spend – big pools winner
Lights Camera Action – Film industry derived
Ready – Steady – Go The classic 'starter'
Money – Money – Money Abba

Even the Church uses it.
Faith, Hope and Charity
The Father, the Son and the Holy Ghost
I am the way, the truth and the life – Jesus

By using the 'rule of three', you will reinforce the belief in your statements and invoke an action. It also makes life easier for your customer or audience. Most people can only remember three facts so make sure you state the ones you want remembered, clearly.

Winston Churchill is famously remembered for his **Blood, Sweat and Tears** speech when in fact it was Blood, Sweat, Toil and Tears, but we can only remember three so it became shortened. Adolf Hitler fired the emotions of thousands with his "Sieg Heil, Sieg Heil, Sieg Heil" chants perhaps the most readily recognised as the use of three.

Do you remember going to the local shops as a child with a list of things to buy and you only ever remembered the first three? Adults do the same thing. Deliver facts in threes.

CHAPTER FIFTEEN

EMOTIONAL TRIGGERS

The art of closing is to act as a catalyst to a decision NOW. How do you get that prospect who is just not making a decision into the frame of mind where they want to go ahead?

You can spur potential customers into action by using emotional triggers. It is important to appeal to your customers on an emotional level because as I have said they will buy through emotion and not logic.

Here are my Top Ten Emotional triggers

1 Value

Value is hot on the agenda for everyone today. No one wants to feel they have wasted money. Using phrases such as "and we have a price match policy that means if you can find the same XXXX cheaper within the next seven days, we will match it," is effective at putting someone's mind at rest. Remember though, it must be the truth.

2 Competition

There is an old saying about keeping up with the Jones' and that still holds good today. Make their tongues hang out for your product and then tell them that they are probably the first amongst their friends to own one. They want to be equal or better than their peers.

3 Trend - setting

Many people want to be trendy or cool, so appeal to that emotion during your presentation. Find the trigger with your product that will put them ahead of the pack. Build on their need to be cool.

4 Belonging

Another big emotional trigger is wanting to belong to the group. Wanting to 'fit in'. Does your company have a mission with its product or service. People want to be a part of the family, tell exactly that – they are joining your 'family' unit.

5 Trust

Trust is one of the hottest emotional triggers in sales and marketing. Using phrases like 'no hidden fees' 'everything is clearly written down for you' and 'This means you don't have to worry' can be key to securing the order. Make them feel confident that you can deliver on your promises.

6 Instant Gratification

We live in a 'now' world. It took my grandmother four hours to cook a Sunday roast. My mother had a better oven and did cooked it in three hours. My wife's oven will cook the same sized joint in under two hours but some people use a microwave oven that takes 20 minutes and they are standing there looking at their watch and saying "come on, hurry up."

Use phrases like "Within twenty four hours", "Delivery today", words like "Today," "Now" and "Straight away" for maximum impact.

7 Leadership

Many consumers want to lead the way with new products. They respond to a message that highlights leadership. Use phrases that make them feel they are first, such as – "they would be the first in the street." These will make them feel in control of the events and are powerful calls to action. Courage is another good tag – "it takes courage to show the others the way" and watch their shoulders go back with pride.

8 Fear

Fear can be widely used whatever your product or service.

Fear of Loss – once they can see themselves in ownership of your product they don't want to lose it. Point out the cost of saying No rather than them dwelling on the cost of saying Yes. Make them see both sides of the decision. Fear of non – ownership. Roadside Assistance companies talk about "don't break down without proper cover. Don't let your family go unprotected."

9 Guilt

Similar in concept to the Fear factor. To be effective you need to focus on the people who rely on them. "What will happen when ...., how will you feel?" Your family rely on you to do the right thing and provide them with the best you can afford. Don't let them think you don't care.

10 Time

People are so busy today. They don't have much spare time. That is why internet shopping is growing. It's quick and easy. Point out they have better things to do than keep searching – Nike have the right slogan – Just Do It!

Emotional triggers work because they invoke an action, but you have to say them in a conversational manner. This is the time for soft, encouraging words. Be almost conspiratorial.

Ideally these triggers are used when you are side by side with your prospect, in other words in a non-confrontational position. You are tugging at their very 'insides' so be kind and the results will come. Be harsh and they will cause antagonism.

Tapping into the Emotions of your customers is also one of the most effective ways of gaining their trust, so make sure you don't say anything to destroy that feeling.

TASK

Write down ten emotional triggers, one for each category, that you could effectively use for your sales presentation.

Share them with your Practice Buddy and see how each one would make them feel.

Ask yourself if you would react to any of them, and until the answer is "Yes," keep searching.

CHAPTER SIXTEEN

CLOSING FOR PROFIT

Read this carefully. Think about the answer.

Do not turn to the next page until you have answered the question.

You own a point of sale, maybe a shop or website which has no overheads or costs of sale. No rent, commissions or taxes to pay. Your profit is yours.

You buy an item for £10 and then sell it for £15.

Have you made a profit? Yes or No

Explain your answer.

No cheating. Write down your explanation before you turn the page.

THE ANSWER IS NO

You haven't made a profit until you can replace it for less than £15. If the price had gone up and it cost £15 to replace, then you haven't made profit you have simply cashed in your stock. If it costs £18 to replace you haven't made a loss, simply cashed in your stock. If you can restock at £10 you have made a £5 profit.

Selling is no different.

You have a lead or prospect. You make a presentation with them, they say yes and you close the deal. You haven't really made a profit yet, just 'cashed in' your lead.

How about replacing that lead for nothing? Ask for a referral and explain why they are so important to you. Wouldn't they have loved to have had a recommendation from a friend so that they knew they could trust the person they were dealing with?

Explain that it doesn't have to be people who are in the market right now, what you like to do is expand your potential customer base by writing a short letter introducing yourself and your company with a business card. You want to use their name as a point of reference so that when that person is in the market in thefuture, they would come and see you first.

There is a bonus in this for your customer too.

Tell them openly that if they have recommended you and people are likely to ask their opinion after delivery or fitting, then it really guarantees they will get a smooth ride and a great job.

That is true, but there is also an added advantage for you.

Having given their friends names, (and you must write to them straight away), they are very unlikely to cancel and now have to admit to their friends that they wanted new sofas but having ordered them changed their minds and are sticking with the old ones.

Everyone will know it was a case of not being able to afford it

They will not cancel their deal!

Plus you have the bonus of getting perhaps one or two more leads and that means you really have made a profit. You 'sold' a lead and replaced it for nothing – now that is great business.

This is also an important part of our next subject, making sure your deal sticks and you stop buyers' remorse.

CONSOLIDATION

This is the most important part of any closing sequence.

What would be the point of closing the deal only to find that it is cancelled the following day? Getting the referral is a great way to consolidate too, but stick to these rules and your deals will stick. Close it and make sure it stays closed.

Don't rush away.

What you say after the deal is closed is worth ten times whatever you said during the sale. Play nicely. Congratulate them by sharing in them imagining using their purchase.

Don't give anything else away.

I have watched too many sales people give extras at this point. Your deal is closed – keep it that way.

Stay as the same person.

Don't become a different character. Very often, the salesperson changes their 'personality' after the sale is done. Make sure you stay in the same character – that is the person they bought from, so stay that way.

Finally, don't overstay your welcome.

Don't rush away but don't settle in for the duration either.
Be sensible, be polite and be effective.
Know when to leave as any good guest does.

TASK

YOUR MOST IMPORTANT PRESENTATION AND CLOSE

There is one prospect you have to close every day and that is You. If you really want to be the top closer in your company and really make the big rewards then complete this task and re- read this page every day. Copy the questions and answers onto a 6x4 card and carry it with you, tape a copy onto the reverse of your sun visor and look at it before every presentation. It is Your WHY.

<u>Answer the following questions on a separate sheet of paper.</u>

Why are you in your current profession?
Why are you with your present Company?
Are you the Number One producer?
If the answer is "No", then what would you have to do to become the Number One producer, every sales period?
What difference would being Number One make to you?
How much more income would you achieve?
What would you do with that income?
Are you prepared to do what it takes?
Sign the sheet to say Yes.

We have agreed that the truth is vital to success and you cannot lie to yourself, otherwise the whole deal is a waste of time. If you are really ready to turn yourself into a professional closer then once you have answered all of the above questions, in writing, you can move on to the next page and begin the process of getting to the very peak of fitness as a professional.

Warning. If you look at the next page to see what you have to do, before your sign the sheet, then you will not succeed. You have to agree to 'whatever it takes' and mean it. Be truthful to you.

THE TESTIMONIAL

If you use the product or service you are selling then develop your own testimonial story. It has to be truthful.
Nothing is more powerful than a personal success story. Again, if you are just starting out, tell the story about why you are involved with your company. "Why did you choose them?" " What was it about their products or service that made you want to work with them?"

Borrow the story of one of your more experienced colleagues that appeals to you. Tell your prospect the truth, this was told to you by a colleague, and it impressed you enough to get involved yourself.

Now tell the truth. Make the point that they will make a decision to buy from this company or use their service once. You make that decision several times every day. If there was a company with better products at the same price or the same product or service at a lesser price, then you would be working for them. The reason why you are selling for this company is that you haven't found anyone else to compare.

TASK

Write down testimonials about the following:
Why you bought the car you are driving?
Why you chose the last place you went on holiday.
What is your favourite restaurant or bar? Why?
What was it about your house that made you buy it?
Produce two other examples of your own.

Ideally they will relate to the product or service you are involved with and you can then use them.

PART SEVEN

BECOME A PROFESSIONAL

NO ATHLETE WOULD COMPETE AND EXPECT TO WIN WITHOUT KEEPING TO A STRICT TRAINING ROUTINE AND HAVING A WARM UP PROCEDURE.

PROFESSIONALS NEVER STOP TRAINING

CHAPTER SEVENTEEN

Congratulations on getting to here, but reading this book is not enough. You need to learn the closes, which are simply mini–presentations in their own right, and then practice, practice and practice them again and again, until they become a reflex action as a part of your selling skills. By constant rehearsal and repetition, they will form an integral part of your conversation as any catch phrase does.

Remember the rule of three and practice three at a time until you know them inside out and upside down. When the time comes to use them you will be confident and quietly strong and that makes a good closer.

As a professional (someone who is paid for what they do) you are part of a profession that can hold its head high because it drives every industry in the world.
No matter what is made or whatever service is offered, unless someone goes out and sells it, then there are no jobs for the people who make it or provide it. Every business relies on the ability of its sales force – we are the engine room that provides the power for business to move forward.

The professional closer does not allow previous successes or results to determine the outcome of their present meeting. Amateurs all too often do exactly that, in fact they even let their private life determine the outcome of their business day

Just imagine. You have a bad morning at home, perhaps a row with your partner so you are feeling grumpy and aggressive. You get to your first appointment and let your customer have it with both barrels in order to get it off your chest. Would you expect to close that sale? No of course not.

What if you are feeling sad at news you have received earlier. Your voice lacks any energy or enthusiasm, in fact you are like a wet blanket. Do you expect to close the next pitch you do? No of course not.

The professional has a switch they throw, as does any performer, athlete or even barrister.

They are prepared, rehearsed and ready to go at a moments notice and use a switch like the ignition key in a car. I remember a good friend who was a well known opera singer. He exuded emotion and power on stage. He could invoke laughter or tears, joy or pathos by his performance. Before he performed he would make up, dress and then begin a warm up routine for his voice. He would never sing ‘cold’.

He would ‘walk the part’ in his dressing room and on his way to the wings ready to walk on to that stage. At the very last moment he would rotate the diamond ring on his finger until it was pointing outward and then punch his other palm again and again until he almost drew blood. That was his signal to roar into life and the moment he walked out under the lights he was on form. An amazing man.

Watch professional sportsmen. In golf every professional has a pre–round routine and a pre–shot routine. The best players in the world spend at least an hour warming up on the practice ground. They work through every club in the bag in exactly the same order every time. Hey build a swing tempo and routine. Then they walk to the putting green and practice there for another twenty or thirty minutes until they are ready to walk to the first tee.

Amateurs want to arrive at the clubhouse, dash in for a quick coffee and then change their shoes and go right to the first tee. They swish a driver a few times and then expect to hit their best shot. Amateur is not the word. In fact when someone comments “amateur” it becomes a derogatory term.

The Pro has a pre–shot routine that switches their mind and body on to the shot they are about to make. They visualise the flight and shape of the shot. They see it land and then they trust their muscle memory to deliver the required shot.

We all need a similar pre–event routine if we want to deliver our best results every time.

When you get dressed for work, think of yourself as a performer on stage. Who would believe you playing a Viking warrior in a suit? Who would believe you playing a High Court Judge in jeans and a tee shirt? Dress for success. Dress in the way that you fit the role of the person you are portraying. Make sure you feel good. If you do business in jeans and a polo shirt make sure they are clean and pressed. Feel great.

If you are travelling to your appointments, make sure you have good music in the car. Sing along. Sing loud to get your voice working. Maybe play CDs that improve your skills or get you in that positive frame of mind.

Why are you doing your job? Who is dependent on your income? If it's your child or children, then stick a photograph of your family on the sun visor and make sure you turn it down and take a good look before you get out of the car. Get into the right frame of mind. A good picture will make you smile warmly and put you in a great place mentally, and that will always benefit your results. You will also feel better.

Walk tall. You are great! You have a great proposition to offer and you know that it will benefit your prospect. You are honest in your pitch and have nothing to be ashamed of. Who would not be proud to be a member of your chosen profession?

There will be people who have a pre–conceived idea of a sales person. Often it will have been gained either by previous experience or through gossip and rumour from others. That is their challenge not yours.

Ask them if they have ever been to an event, film or party that they really were not looking forward to because of a preconceived idea of what it would be like? Have they ever then been pleasantly surprised and enjoyed themselves because it wasn't like that at all? They would never have known if they didn't go and see for themselves.

Ask them, "Why not treat this conversation the same way. You think I am a particular kind of person and that I will conduct myself in a set way. I promise you I am not like that but why not tell me afterwards how you feel?"

Now do EXACTLY the same presentation as always. Do not change your format to suit the person you are pitching because if you do you will have no yardstick to work from.

The reverse is also true.

Never pre–judge a sales prospect. The amount of times every experienced professional has started a pitch, thinking that they are wasting their time, only to be pleasantly surprised at the outcome when they closed the deal would amaze you!

However if you prejudge and then cut short your presentation for that reason, then you will not be successful and will have contributed to a self–prophesied failure.

Every presentation must be delivered in its entirety, with energy and enthusiasm, otherwise you are wasting your time.

Closing skills will never make up for a poor presentation. In fact the best close, is a well delivered presentation to a qualified prospect, that will close itself. Perfection.

Finally, you have a practice buddy, now extend that scenario.

Form a Mastermind Group of people with a genuine desire to progress in their field. They don't necessarily have to come from your profession but they should be entrepreneurial in their outlook and always looking to improve their performance.

Find a coach or join a coaching programme even if it is online and you can participate in webinars or conference call trainings. Never stop learning.

Listen to CDs in the car. Watch DVDs or online videos. Build a library that not only you use to progress but may become the basis of your teaching programme when you move into a position of leadership as you surely will as your results improve and you start winning the recognition of your peers. Go into any lawyer's office and you will see their library. You should be collecting your reference points as you grow.

Start a success book. Keep a record of all the things that make you feel good or bring a smile to your face. It can be the smallest thing; it can be a business success. The item may only be a five word entry or it may be a page. Every time you are about to enter the presentation arena, take a moment to open your success book and remember how it felt when you did that special thing that made you feel so good. Then, whilst you are in that frame of mind, go and get another success.

I have a mantra: **"Excuses are not acceptable."** Try it.

"No one is responsible for my success and no one should take responsibility for my failures. Everything is in my control."
You are now in control of your sales future. Enjoy it!

SHARE THIS BOOK WITH OTHERS

To purchase books online go to www.larrybrooks.co.uk.
Send an email to larry@larrybrooks.co.uk
or telephone 01753 664455 during office hours

If you wish to purchase books in bulk for your organisation,
call to discuss the bulk discounts available.

Books can also be specially printed and customised
for your company or organisation.
For information, e–mail your contact details and
the prospective quantities you require.

Why not book Larry as a Guest Speaker for Your next Conference or Seminar?

Go to www.larrybrooks.co.uk and complete the details of your conference or seminar, and your organisation or team can enjoy anything from an hour to a full day.

If you are interested in One to One Personal Coaching, send your full details to larry@larrybrooks.co.uk

ABOUT THE AUTHOR

For forty years, Larry Brooks has coached and trained people in Selling, Closing and Presentation Skills. As a speaker at seminars across the globe, across the UK and Europe, Japan, USA, Canada, and the Middle East, Larry has a reputation as someone who speaks from first hand experience and a knowledge of exactly what works.
He has coached individuals who wanted to be the very best and spoken to audiences of up to 55,000 people, in a packed out baseball stadium.
Close the Deal highlights his solidly founded skill set and the coaching style that has made a difference to so many entrepreneurs and sales professionals, and now you can share these highly effective presentations and guidelines to success.
In just a few hours you can start to change your results and the ensuing rewards. Ask yourself; "If I was to close twice as many sales presentations what difference would that make to my way of life?" Is that possible? Yes it is. Read and study this book and tomorrow really can be the day your results improve dramatically and your rewards change forever.

Send your comments on the book to larry@larrybrooks.co.uk

A FINAL THOUGHT.

Have you ever read Alice in Wonderland? Most people would describe the book as a fairy story, but in reality it is a book of pure adult logic, written in a way that children can understand.

For example, Alice starts to cry because she is tired and lost. Cheshire Cat is sitting in the tree, grinning. Alice asks, "I am lost and I don't know where to go. Which path should I take?"

Cheshire Cat replies, "That all depends where you want to go." Alice says "I don't really mind where." Cheshire Cat says, "Then it doesn't really matter which path you choose" "But I want to get there in the end," says Alice. "And you will," says Cheshire Cat, "If you keep walking long enough."

We will all arrive at various points in our life. Do you want to choose yours or let 'chance' be your guide?

The Queen of Hearts is baking tarts, sprinkling pepper all around the room, and that is making the baby cry. The Queen is angry and tells Alice to get the baby to sleep and be quiet. "How do I do that?" asks Alice. "Tell it a story." says the Queen. "What sort of story?" enquired Alice.
"I don't know, any kind of story that will make it sleep and be quiet," said the Queen. "Where should I begin?" pleads Alice. The Queen says profoundly, "Begin at the beginning and end at the end. How else would you tell a story?"

Simple isn't it? Begin at the beginning and end at the end. Then, when you reach the end, you should close the book.

This is the end of the book and the start of your new journey. If you learn and practice the contents, you can determine Your own level of success and satisfaction. Enjoy.